Instructor's Manual

LITERATURE AND SOCIETY

Instructor's Manual

LITERATURE AND SOCIETY

An Introduction to Fiction, Poetry, Drama, Nonfiction

———————— Second Edition ————————

PAMELA J. ANNAS
University of Massachusetts/Boston

ROBERT C. ROSEN
William Paterson College

Prentice Hall
Englewood Cliffs, New Jersey 07632

© 1994 by PRENTICE-HALL, INC.
A Paramount Communications Company
Englewood Cliffs, N.J. 07632

10 9 8 7 6 5 4 3 2 1

ISBN 0-13-532920-5
Printed in the United States of America

CONTENTS

GROWING UP AND GROWING OLDER / 1

FICTION

POETRY

DRAMA

NONFICTION

WOMEN AND MEN / 33

FICTION

POETRY

DRAMA

NONFICTION

MONEY AND WORK / 68

DRAMA

NONFICTION

PEACE AND WAR / 100

FICTION

POETRY

DRAMA

NONFICTION

VARIETIES OF PROTEST / 132

FICTION

POETRY

DRAMA

NONFICTION

GROWING UP AND GROWING OLDER

The short fiction in this section is arranged chronologically by life stages. We would like to suggest ways the drama, nonfictional prose, and featured poems also fit into these life stages. The excerpt from Brave New World is a satiric vision of birth and, along with "Battle Royal," "Girl," and the excerpt from The Bluest Eye, is about social conditioning. The Whitman, Lorde, Ortiz, and two Hayden poems, also about childhood, fit here. "Battle Royal," "Girl," and the chapter from A Boy's Own Story focus on the entry into adolescence. The two nonfictional prose pieces, by Maxine Hong Kingston and Audre Lorde, are also at this life stage. Baldwin's "Sonny's Blues" and Hawthorne's "Young Goodman Brown" are located at the transition from adolescence into adulthood, at the point one's identity has to begin to come to terms with the larger world. Sylvia Plath's Three Women (in the drama section) is about pregnancy and childbirth, as are the Ostriker, Dericotte, and Olds poems. T.S. Eliot's "The Love Song of J. Alfred Prufrock" moves us into middle age, as do the Clifton, Justice, and Updike poems, and perhaps also Irena Klepfisz's "they did not build wings for them," a poem which challenges stereotypes of the spinster. King Lear and Krapp's Last Tape are about old age, as is the Mary E. Wilkins Freeman story, "A Mistaken Charity." The Yeats and Shakespeare poems and Judith Ortiz Cofer's "Old Women" fit here as well. Check out notes on the additional poems in this manual for further exploration of each of these life stages. Wordsworth's ". . . Tintern Abbey" and Harjo's "Remember" are more philosophical explorations.

Depending on the age of your students, you might choose to focus on one or another of these life stages. Or you might wish to move through all of them. More lively discussion will probably take place concerning life stages students have had some chance to experience themselves, and we would caution against choosing primarily to focus on the stage the instructor is at rather than where the students are. They might be bored; you might be embarrassed. On the other hand, if you can get even younger students to think about middle and old age in terms of their parents' and grandparents' lives, that would give them a way into such texts and a way of connecting their own life observations with the literature.

We find that asking students to write autobiographically — even in literature courses — is useful in giving them an understanding from the inside of how writers work: how they choose a central focus and develop characters, a plot, images. Here you might ask them to choose an incident from a life stage they have already passed through and write about it.

FICTION

Aldous Huxley, from Brave New World

You might begin by asking students to describe as fully as possible the society depicted, to infer as much as they can about it from these first two chapters of the novel. Perhaps the next question to ask is exactly what is <u>wrong</u> with this society. (Play devil's advocate. Near the end of the novel, the Resident World Controller for Western Europe says that people "get what they want, and. . . never want what they can't get." Isn't this happiness?) Students may say that the problem is that this society is not like our society. So it might be worth focusing next on what kinds of trends in our society the excerpt seems to be extrapolating (and satirizing): the equating of progress with technological and material progress, the subordination of people to the needs of the economy (training children to hate nature so they'll consume sporting equipment), the destruction of individuality and the manipulation of the populace, and so on. Growing up, for us, involves being socialized and resisting that socialization; parents, religious institutions, schools help mold us into 'more productive members of society,' often at the expense of our own needs. But this dialectic is missing in the world of <u>Brave New World</u>; the needs of the 'individual' and the needs of society (as determined by those in power) are the same. What enables Huxley's dystopian vision still to engage us today is not his projection into the future of technological trends (his biology seems rather crude in an age of genetic engineering) but his projection of social and political trends. The kind of perfectly stable, stratified, pacified society he depicts would solve many of the problems today's world leaders (in the private as well as the public sectors) feel themselves burdened with. (P.S.: Don't forget to ask students if they find Huxley <u>funny</u>.)

Ralph Ellison, "Battle Royal"

Though metaphor, symbol, and irony are essential to this story, it is important first to be sure students can make sense of it on a realistic level. It is ironic that the "town's leading white citizens" abuse and humiliate the narrator and then give him a scholarship, and it is ironic that despite this abuse he wants their approval; but there is a logic to the situation: it makes sense politically and psychologically. They reward him not just for his academic abilities but for how much he's willing to swallow (the metaphors are hard to escape); they're convincing themselves that "some day he'll lead his people in the proper paths." They abuse him not only for their amusement but also to let him know that they're in charge, that the alternative to being their 'house slave' is unpleasant indeed. And he wants their approval because getting it represents his only chance to continue his education. The battle royal and the electrified rug have rich symbolic value; within the world of the story, they teach the young men their place in society. The white men enjoy the spectacle for many reasons, but probably most because it 'proves' to them that blacks (and women, too) are as low as they always thought. In light of all this, the deathbed advice of the grandfather — "overcome'em with yeses. . . agree'em to death and destruction" —seems more a comforting illusion than a plan of action; the story he tells in the narrator's dream seems more to the point.

Jamaica Kincaid, "Girl"

This is a good piece (it has been variously described as an essay, a short story, and a prose poem) to use to help students understand voice. And a useful exercise, after discussing "Girl," is to ask students to write a piece modeled on this one that captures the voice of socialization they heard and probably internalized growing up. The trick here is to take different pieces of advice they got — from parents, teachers, media — and create one consistent voice that has a theme and that isn't a random collection. In "Girl," the center is growing up female in this particular island culture. A discussion of the story usually brings up the issue of social class. What social class is this "girl"? How do we know that? How old is she? Answers range from 7 to 17, but we'd guess about eleven to thirteen. In the two (italicized) responses the girl makes, she doesn't seem to understand her mother's worries about sexuality and social class; i.e., that she will grow up to be a tramp instead of a lady. If students do try a page or two modelled on "Girl" and drawn from their own lives, they can begin with gender (how was I raised as a boy, as a girl), but region will soon come in (American midwest, southern, northern urban, etc), as will social class (working class — urban or rural? — suburban middle class, old American money, whatever), race and ethnicity (the voices that socialize you if you're black in this country have different things to say than if you are white, similarly if Latino, Asian, Native American, Jewish, Italian, etc., etc.). Ask students to, like Kincaid, include as many vivid details as possible. And to keep a consistent characterization in the voice they create. Students might also think about what categories of practical advice Kincaid's girl is given: household tasks, superstitions, social relations up and down the class ladder, self image (dress and behavior), in some sense how to be happy and maintain your equanimity and serenity.

Toni Morrison, from <u>The Bluest Eye</u>

The Bluest Eye (1970) is Toni Morrison's first novel and for sheer gorgeousness of language has not been surpassed in any of her subsequent work. This excerpt will be an interesting introduction to the book for students who are familiar with Morrison, if at all, through her more recent fiction. The Bluest Eye is in part "about" the incestuous rape of a barely adolescent girl, Pecola, who becomes pregnant, delivers a stillborn child, and goes crazy (it is not clear in which order the last two happen). So the novel has received bad press as being about the pathology of the Black community. And yet the perspective of the novel is that of another young girl, Claudia, whose voice we hear in the excerpt included here. Claudia is anything but a victim. Her healthy self assertion, her appropriate anger, and her questioning intelligence are in evidence here in the Christmas baby doll section, which is one episode layered among several episodes in this chapter.

The Bluest Eye spans a year in the lives of three young African-American girls, Claudia (the narrator), and her sister Frieda, and Pecola, who sometimes stays with them as a short-term foster child. A major concern of the novel is social class in the Black and White communities and we see examples of several "families" which embody particular class situations.

Central to this novel is the issue of how a child, specifically here an African-American female child, constructs an identity. What does the culture you live in hold up to you as appropriate role models or as repositories for your affection? Here the icon is a big, white, blue-eyed baby doll and Claudia hates it. What values and assumptions are being presented to her in the form of this doll? In what specific ways are these assaults on her identity — as a child, as a girl, as an African-American? How is her response a healthy one?

Students enjoy discussing this prose piece, especially if they can be helped to identify with Claudia by remembering ways in which they themselves were pressured into (socialized into) certain roles and certain attitudes about themselves and others —perhaps also through Christmas or birthday gifts. Jamaica Kincaid's "Girl" works well alongside this story.

Edmund White, from <u>A Boy's Own Story</u>

Along with the excerpts in this section from Audre Lorde's <u>Zami</u> and Maxine Hong Kingston's <u>The Woman Warrior</u>, White's piece is a useful example of autobiographical writing focused on the agonizing entry into adolescence. White's, of course, is from a male perspective and it might be interesting for students to compare male and female experiences of that time of life, not only in these stories but in their own lives. The three also provide different forms for organizing one's experience in autobiographical writing: Kingston's centers on an instructional and frightening tale her mother told her; Lorde's uses a remembered artifact, the mortar and pestle, to structure her memories of puberty; White's, more episodic and linear, is organized around two issues: popularity (including friendship, romance and love) and sexual identity.

For a young male unsure of his sexual identity, as White's narrator is, unsure whether he is primarily attracted to boys or to girls, the entry into adolescence must be even more confusing than it is already. Compare the solidity and reality of the narrator's friendship with Tom, even though the implications of his feelings disturb him, with the unreality, almost artificiality, of his date and subsequent "crush" on Helen, even though that is what he's "supposed" to be feeling and doing. Beyond the particular circumstances of this narrator is the question of peer group pressure to conform and, standing behind that, the social norms for conformity. Whatever our individual circumstances, we can all probably remember from this period of our lives (approximately ages 12 - 16) the confusions of our emerging sexuality and personality and the bewildering availability of advice about what to do with all of it.

Autobiographical writing is a compelling way to get students engaged in the writing process. You might ask students to write about some incident in their early adolescence that captures for them (and hopefully for their readers) the quality of and the major issues in their lives then.

James Baldwin, "Sonny's Blues"

Students — especially if they don't quite make it to the end — may tend to read a simple anti-drug message into this story and (if they are not black) may also see in it confirmation of certain racial stereotypes. But the story is more about music than about heroin, which is, in any case, primarily a symptom, not a cause, of Sonny's anguish. The effects of racism are at the heart of the story; it's important not to forget the Sunday afternoon gatherings of the narrator's childhood, when fear would descend on the room, or the story his mother told him of how his father's brother was killed. Sonny has tried to cope with his and his community's suffering by transforming it into art; practicing at the piano, he is "playing for his life." The narrator has tried to escape his community, has set up emotional barriers between himself and the suffering of those like Sonny, has tried to insulate himself from black people who do not share his (seemingly) safe and stable middle-class existence. The drama of the story lies in the narrator's breaking out of the conventional attitudes and emotional defenses that alienate him from his community. It is the older brother who grows, the teacher who learns.

Nathaniel Hawthorne, "Young Goodman Brown"

Like several of Hawthorne's stories, and reflecting his New England Puritan upbringing, "Young Goodman Brown" is about the encounter of innocence with evil. What do students think about the degree of young Goodman Brown's naiveté? A possible writing exercise might be for students to update the story, retelling it in contemporary terms — either straight or satirically.

Since Hawthorne's subject is often innocence encountering evil, we might ask how innocence fares in this story. What is Hawthorne's view in "Young Goodman Brown" of human nature? How does he chip away at his hero's naiveté through the story? What are the stages of Brown's loss of innocence/coming to knowledge? How does Brown struggle against this new view of the world that is being forced upon him?

Students might consider the narrative devices of the journey and the dream that Hawthorne employs. In some ways, Brown's night in the forest is a compressed version of the whole of a human life, with its gradual disillusionments. The possibility that it was all a dream underlines the uncertainty of our visions of morality. How can we know that any of what we believe is accurate — whether our view of human nature is optimistic or pessimistic. How does young Goodman Brown live the rest of his life in the face of this uncertainty?

In another sense, this is a fable about growing up and having one's idealism confront and come to terms with the world's realities. We might ask: is what Brown encounters during his journey reality, or is it just another way of looking at the world? How do we, as individuals, cope with taking in new information that challenges our world view? Do we reject it, integrate it, or let it turn our world upside down? What does young Goodman Brown do?

Mary E. Wilkins Freeman, "A Mistaken Charity"

A story about old age, about women, about being poor and working class, about coping with disability, "A Mistaken Charity" can be approached in a number of ways. A television dramatization of the story was produced recently and, if that is available, you could talk about the two mediums of print and video and issues of adaptation. As a story about the traditionally powerless, "A Mistaken Charity" is popular with students because the protagonists have a lot of fighting spirit and win in the end — though we don't know, of course, what might happen to them next.

We have sometimes taught this story along with Alice Walker's "Everyday Use" as an exploration of cross-class encounters, between the working class and the middle class. In Walker's story, the tension is between a working-class mother and her upwardly mobile daughter. And Mary E. Wilkins Freeman, writing eighty or so years before Walker, focuses on an encounter between members of different social classes within an established small town community. In both these stories, authorial sympathy is with the working-class characters, all of whom demonstrate working-class pride and triumph in the end.

8

What meanings accrue to the word "charity" in Freeman's story? To what extent are the providers of the "mistaken" charity acting out of mistaken assumptions about what is good for the recipients of their benevolence? To what extent are their assumptions structured by their social class position?

Leslie Marmon Silko, "Lullaby"

Since the story is told through Ayah's eyes, we are quickly made aware — through her metaphors, and through the intense detail of her observation — of her deep connection to nature. As embodied in the lullaby at the end, this relationship to an unchanging (and generally benevolent) natural world has given her the strength to endure all she has had to endure, and even comforts her as she faces likely death (at nature's hand!) at the end. The white world, by contrast, may have saved her children Danny and Ella from death, but at the cost of isolating them from their community and Ayah from them. The white world has also taken the life of her son Jimmie, and the soul of her husband Chato, who has imitated "their" ways and gotten nothing for it. Time has made Ayah stronger but Chato only weaker, as well as a "stranger" now to his wife of forty years. After the white doctors took the children away, Ayah "did not lie down beside Chato again" for many years, not only because, as she says, he "had taught her to sign her name" (and thus, unwittingly, to sign away her children), but also, we suspect, because the thought of having more children (who, one way or another, might also be taken away) was just too painful. Yet, at the end, she takes Chato back, and comforts him, perhaps recognizing him now not as her enemy but as her fellow victim. Her deepest needs are not to separate but to connect, as she sings to Chato and to her lost children the lullaby that her grandmother and mother had sung.

POETRY

Walt Whitman, "We Two Boys Together Clinging"

This poem captures the strength, spontaneity, and rebelliousness of youthful joy — even "air breathing" is worth celebrating. The two boys have no responsibility but to discover themselves and the world, "No law less than ourselves owning." The structure of the single sentence that makes up the poem keeps the reader moving along quickly and creates a strong sense of endless activity. (Since there's neither rhyme nor meter, students might be asked what makes this poetry.) Given the biographical note on Whitman, there might be some discussion of that "loving." This is one of Whitman's Calamus poems —about "adhesiveness, manly love," as he put it. It is about love and camaraderie in some abstract sense (there's no description of the other boy) and at the same time more specifically about gay male love, though the poem obviously comes from a more repressive era than our own.

Audre Lorde, "From the House of Yemanjá"

This poem is from Lorde's 1978 volume, The Black Unicorn. A poem about parent/child and especially mother/daughter relations, this could be read along with Kincaid's "Girl" and Roethke's "My Papa's Waltz." Also note the prose selection (from Zami) by Lorde in this section. Even more specifically, the poem centers upon the difficult and ambivalent situation of growing up black in a white and racist society. Children from oppressed groups in a society have to be acculturated in two ways simultaneously: into the values and mores of the dominant culture and their place in it and also into some positive sense of their own identity. Thus the mother here is seen double —"one dark and rich and hidden/in the ivory hungers of the other/mother/pale as a witch." What this produces in the daughter is a curious kind of double identity, an identity located on the knife edge between them, which is a tense and uncomfortable place to spend one's life. W.E.B. DuBois in The Souls of

Black Folk (1903) gave a name to this phenomenon: "It is a peculiar sensation, this double-consciousness, this sense of always looking at oneself through the eyes of others." However, there is a survivor's strength that can come out of this tension and it is apparent in the images of the poem. In a prose collection, The Cancer Journals, Lorde writes: "I am not only a casualty. I am also a warrior."

Robert Hayden, "Those Winter Sundays" and "The Whipping"

Only now as an adult does the speaker in "Those Winter Sundays" recognize and appreciate what his father did for him, that heating the house and polishing the shoes were acts of love, "austere and lonely," for which "No one ever thanked him." The intense regret in the last two lines (especially in the repetition of "what did I know") suggests that it is now too late for the speaker to thank his father. Students might be asked to infer the social class of the speaker (as a child) and to discuss its consequences.

The speaker of "The Whipping" is also an adult who now better understands a parental figure than he did as a child. The poem shifts point of view twice, beginning with an external description of the whipping as seen "across the way," then (perhaps as the speaker gets more deeply involved in remembering) moving into the boy's point of view ("My head . . . "), and then moving out again to a more external point of view, ending with an explanation of what might have driven the woman to whip the child so fiercely — namely the "lifelong hidings/she has had to bear."

John Updike, "Ex-Basketball Player"

Pearl Avenue, in the first three lines, parallels Flick's career. We see him now as a rather pathetic shadow of his former greatness, his glory still alive only in his fantasy, as he imagines "bright applauding tiers/Of Necco Wafers, Nibs, and Juju Beads." Though Esso is now Exxon and gas pump styles have changed, students relate easily to this poem and usually can talk of someone they know who is like Flick. They may pick up on a certain social class condescension towards Flick; you might ask them to characterize the speaker. This might be followed with a discussion of who or what is to blame for what's happened to Flick.

T.S. Eliot, "The Love Song of J. Alfred Prufrock"

Along with the imagistic "Preludes," this long poem is Eliot's first major work and by some considered his best. Aside from the epigraph in Italian, "Prufrock" is more language accessible than later Eliot works like The Wasteland, The Four Quartets, and "Ash Wednesday," and more subject-accessible as well since it is about a man concerned 1) with aging and 2) with risking an intimate relationship with another person. A good way to begin discussion is by asking if this is indeed a love poem. Another useful question is how old people think Prufrock is. (Answers range from 21 to 70; our guess is that he's close to Eliot's own age at the time, 29 or 30.) Ask students to notice the use of verb tenses in the poem, where the speaker of the poem uses present tense, future tense, and past tense (as well as the conditional). Especially important is when he begins to use past tense at the end of the stanza that begins, "And the afternoon, the evening, sleeps so peacefully!" He says, "in short, I was afraid." That is the turning point or crisis in the poem, where he's let his chance to make contact pass. People do tend to become impatient with Prufrock and why is sometimes a useful topic to explore. This poem might be considered along with other poems about growing old (or middle-aged, depending on what you conclude about Prufrock's age), poems by Yeats, Clifton, Justice, Shakespeare, Cofer, Carpenter, Klepfisz.

William Butler Yeats, "Sailing to Byzantium"

Yeats's fifty-year poetic career stretches from his first volume, Crossways (1889) to Last Poems (1936-1939). The poems fall loosely into three phases: 1) his early lyrical and romantic poems looking backward to Ireland's mythic past (1889-1904); 2) the poems of his political and public period, from about 1910 or a little earlier to somewhere in the 1920s — "An Irish Airman Foresees His Death" and "Easter 1916" (both in this anthology) are examples; and 3) the poems about aging and the poems written out of his own system of mythology (expounded in his book, A Vision) from 1928 or so until his death. "Sailing to Byzantium" is transitional from the second phase to the third. The two worlds of the poem are the public, sensual Ireland and the spiritual, subjective Byzantium. What is interesting is the poem's ambivalence. Once arrived in Byzantium, the poet, now an artifact, a golden bird, sings of temporality, of what is past, or passing, or to come. In Yeats's mystical system, which involves cycles of history interfaced with the phases of the moon, Byzantium's peak of civilization is 1000 B.C., midway between the savagery of Christ's crucifixion and the projected collapse of civilization in the year 2000. Byzantium is also at the full moon or totally subjective phase of Yeats's phases of the moon. Compare this poem with another Yeats poem about aging, "Crazy Jane Talks with the Bishop."

William Shakespeare, "That time of year thou mayst in me behold"

The speaker compares his growing old, in successive quatrains, to trees losing their leaves in autumn, to sunset fading into night, and to a dying fire. He then asserts, in the final couplet, that the nearness of his end intensifies the love felt for him by the person to whom he is speaking. The process of dying is faster in each successive metaphor and, in the third one, more nearly final. This poem is discussed briefly in "How Poetry Works" (under "Figurative Language" and "Rhyme, Resonance, and Repetition"). It might be taught along with Shakespeare's "When my love swears that she is made of truth" (in the "Women and Men" section); that sonnet is also addressed to a younger lover.

Irena Klepfisz, "they did not build wings for them"

Ask students to look up in the dictionary and compare words like "spinster" and "old maid" with "bachelor." Since Klepfisz is redefining in this poem people's conception of a woman who chooses to remain unmarried, a useful discussion could happen about semantics and how words carry political meanings, that is, how giving a group of people a particular name carries along with the label a whole set of attitudes and behaviors. In this poem the women themselves literally break out of the traditional definition. Klepfisz writes "but aloneness was her real distinction." How does the notion of a creative solitude challenge people's notions of an appropriate life, given that psychologists tell us that approximately 75% of the population in this country are extroverts and only 25% introverts? Further, women's role is traditionally seen as serving or nurturing others. These women's independence, solitude, and self nurturance is a further challenge to stereotypes about appropriate ways to spend one's life. Our guess is that, even beyond gender, readers will find the vision of this poem either inviting or distasteful and frightening, depending on whether they are introverted or extroverted.

Joy Harjo, "Remember"

"Remember" is from Harjo's 1983 volume, She Had Some Horses. The chanting cadences and the use of syntactical and other repetition that we see in this poem is characteristic of a number of the poems in that volume, including the title poem. In her next collection, In Mad Love and War (1991), Harjo uses the prose poem form more. The structure here is clear and inviting enough that students might enjoy writing their own "remember" poem. (Any opportunity for students to write some poetry and thereby begin to demystify it is worth noting.) How is this poem an exercise in positioning oneself in the universe and in time? Harjo, as she customarily does, mixes natural and urban imagery, references to Native American and Anglo cultures. Finally the ritual of the poem and the poem as ritual arrive as spiritual wholeness.

William Wordsworth, "Lines Composed a Few Miles Above Tintern Abbey"

There aren't many poems in Literature and Society about nature, and nature, for Wordsworth, is not only apart from society, but also something from which he returns better able to endure society, to suffer "the din/Of towns and cities," amidst which remembrance of nature's beauty has offered him "sensations sweet,/Felt in the blood, and felt along the heart;/And passing even into my purer mind,/With tranquil restoration." Wordsworth marks the stages of his growing up and older in terms not of his relation to the social world but in terms of his relation to nature: from the unconscious "coarser pleasures" and "glad animal movements" of his childhood, to the "passion" and "love" of his youth, to the richer and almost mystical "sense sublime/Of something far more deeply interfused" that he experiences as an adult. The poet's intense connection to nature has not only given him memories to sweeten his days away from nature, but has also made him a better and more knowing person, has informed his "little, nameless, unremembered, acts/Of kindness and of love" and enabled him, at times, to "see into the life of things." And he hopes that soon, for his younger sister Dorothy too, nothing will "disturb/Our cheerful faith, that all which we behold/Is full of blessings." Students might want to discuss whether such a poem could still be written today, when the permanence of natural beauty can no longer so easily be taken for granted.

John Keats, "When I Have Fears"

You might ask students to characterize the fear the speaker describes in each quatrain. What is the logic to the order in which they are described? Is there any way we can read the poem less gloomily than the last line suggests it should be read?

Emily Dickinson, "I'm ceded — I've stopped being Their's"

Rejecting or throwing off the identity she was baptized into as a child, the speaker is now in a sense baptizing herself, "consciously" creating her own identity. Critics have variously interpreted the poem as a celebration of marriage, of newfound and genuine religious faith, of maturity as an artist, or simply of independence. Students may want to debate just what this new baptism represents.

Gerard Manley Hopkins, "Spring and Fall"

Margaret's "ghost" has "guessed" what she cannot yet speak or even consciously think — that we are all mortal — and this, the speaker believes, is why the fallen leaves sadden her. What is the relationship of the speaker to the feelings he attributes to Margaret? Is he projecting his own feelings on her? What are the various meanings of the poem's title? Students may be surprised to see rhyme but nothing that seems like meter.

Hopkins's "sprung rhythm" is based on the number of stressed syllables in a line (here four), irrespective of unstressed syllables.

Renée Vivien, "Whitehaired Women"

How does Vivien characterize these whitehaired women? What do they do? What are they like? How does she work against stereotypes about old women, both in the poem as a whole and in specific phrases and lines like "winter caressed," "flowers of old age," and "you who speak little." This 1904 poem could be compared to Klepfisz's "they did not build wings for them" (1974), which challenges stereotypes about "spinsters," and to Judith Ortiz Cofer's poem "Old Women." You might ask students to imagine themselves old and to write a description of themselves (in either prose or poetry) at, say, age 65 or 75. Renée Vivien herself only lived to age 31; she died in 1909.

Edna St. Vincent Millay, "Grown-up"

This poem is discussed briefly as a lyric in "How Poetry Works." Even college students may imagine and yearn for a future when they will have more freedom —can they anticipate any possible disappointments? Why, in the poem, is the speaker domestic as "a plate"?

Edna St. Vincent Millay, "What Lips My Lips Have Kissed"

This lyric might be read alongside Renée Vivien's "Whitehaired Women." How old do students think the speaker is? Why are those lads "unremembered"? What are the implications of the speaker's comparing herself to a tree in winter?

e.e. cummings, "in Just-"

Any e.e. cummings poem provokes questions about his playful punctuation, capitalization, and use of space on the page. How do such techniques in this cummings poem evoke the playfulness of childhood? What time of spring is just spring? Why a balloonman and not some other kind of vendor? You could ask students to come up with word and image combinations of their own to describe a particular season. In discussing this poem, you could ask them to consider how word/images like "mud-/luscious" and "puddle-wonderful" both economically and vividly express a season and a mood and a time of life.

William Butler Yeats, "Crazy Jane Talks with the Bishop"

"Crazy Jane Talks with the Bishop" is the sixth of seven poems Yeats wrote about Crazy Jane. In the first, "Crazy Jane and the Bishop," we learn that her lover Jack the Journeyman is dead; the Bishop (though not yet Bishop then) had condemned their unmarried love ("he, an old book in his fist/Cried that we lived like beast and beast") and banished Jack. In this poem, the Bishop continues to press his case for chastity. Jane is old now, soon to die, and to the Bishop the choice is clear: "a heavenly mansion" or "some foul sty." Crazy Jane denies this opposition. Soul and body are "near of kin"; soul needs body; love needs both. Crazy Jane makes her case in the last stanza, with anatomical arguments and puns on "soul" and "hole." Despite old age and the nearness of death, she rejects the Bishop's promises and threats.

Margaret Walker, "Lineage"

The speaker feels she must live up to her powerful grandmothers, a feeling no doubt intensified by a sense of pride in being black (explored more fully in Walker's poem "For My People" in the "Varieties of Protest" section). What are the "clean words" her grandmothers have to say? What is the answer to the question at the end? Students (black or non-black) will no doubt have much to say about relatives that they have seen (or who have been held up to them) as models they should live up to — and about how such models can be oppressive as well as inspiring.

Gwendolyn Brooks, "A song in the front yard"

You might ask students to describe the girl who is the speaker of this poem: What's her social class? About how old is she? Is she an only child? What's she wearing? How does she spend her time? What do "the charity children" represent to her? What do they represent to her mother? How about her vision of what she wants to be when she grows up? You could ask students to share some of their more outrageous childhood fantasies about what they wanted to be when they grew up. Ask them if they think Brooks successfully captures the voice of a young girl. How does she use language to create this particular voice? In terms both of mother/daughter disagreement and social class issues, you might consider this poem along with Jamaica Kincaid's "Girl."

Theodore Roethke, "My Papa's Waltz"

See discussion in "How Poetry Works."

Dylan Thomas, "Do Not Go Gentle Into That Good Night"

The speaker (here readily identified with Thomas himself) exhorts his father not to accept death but to fight back, as others have — "wise men" who didn't have the impact on the world they'd hoped for ("forked no lightning"), "good men," wild men" (artists, poets), and "grave men" (a pun, like "good night"). The repetition and tight rhyme scheme — the poem is a villanelle — make it somewhat incantatory. Why "gentle" and not "gently"?

Gwendolyn Brooks, "We Real Cool"

See comments in "How Poetry Works." One of Brooks's most anthologized poems, "We Real Cool" gives off an air of bravado and deceptive simplicity but from the beginning it is pretty bleak and by the last line the chilly pain has fully surfaced. What is the effect of: 1) the syntactic repetition; and 2) breaking each line after "we" and in the middle of a sentence? Compare with Brooks's other poem in this section, "A song in the front yard." How is the attitude toward growing up "bad" different in the two poems?

Amiri Baraka, "Preface to a Twenty Volume Suicide Note"

Someone who sets out to write a twenty-volume suicide note clearly is not serious about committing suicide. The images of death, loss, despair give way to the image of the speaker's daughter talking to an imaginary friend in her hands; perhaps her youth redeems his weariness, and her imagination inspires him again as a poet.

Sylvia Plath, "Edge"

Plath wrote this poem the week before she killed herself in February 1963. Don't be surprised if suicide becomes a main focus of the class discussion. "Edge" in particular draws that response from readers because of its sensuous evocation of death. The mood of the poem is calm, slow, peaceful and you might discuss how the rhythm of the lines and the sound of the words achieve this mood, as in "The illusion of a Greek necessity/Flows in the scrolls of her toga." How does the opening one-line sentence set up the theme of the poem? What does Plath mean by "perfected"? You might discuss how the "characters" in the poem — the woman, the children, the moon —merge with the setting. Two extended metaphors in the poem are the dead woman and children 1) as sculpture and 2) as a closing flower. What is the relation of the moon to all this? Compare the attitude toward death in "Edge" to that in Dylan Thomas's "Do Not Go Gentle Into That Good Night."

Donald Justice, "Men at Forty"

Students at twenty, men or women, may have some trouble relating to this poem, but you might begin by inviting them to talk about moments they've been intensely conscious of being older than they'd once been. Justice's poem describes a heightened awareness of the passage of time and of the finiteness of one's existence, of rooms one won't be "Coming back to," a sense that one's past probably holds more years than one's future ("More fathers than sons themselves now"). At certain moments there's a certain queasiness, but it's still "gentle"; the woods are "filling," but far from full; forty is only the beginning of the end. The mood of the poem is rather wistful — until the last line, when the word "mortgaged" drops on us. Is it that men at forty (at least the married, middle-class, suburban men the poem speaks of) are living on borrowed money as well as borrowed time? Or that the press of mundane problems (charitably?) leaves little time for intimations of mortality. You might ask students to write variations on this poem: "Women at Forty"; "Single Men at Forty"; "Unemployed Men at Forty"; "Women at Sixty." Or even parodies.

Nikki Giovanni, "Woman Poem"

As with all poems, read this or have students read it out loud, paying attention to where the lines break. For a discussion of line breaks as sound cues, see "How Poetry Works." As well as being about being a woman, as the title suggests, "Woman Poem" is about being black and being poor. How do race and social class combine with gender to define this speaker's experience of adolescence and young adulthood? Ask students to list components of the speaker's "unhappiness." What are the relations between people in the speaker's world and what are the socio-economic factors that structure those relations? Notice Giovanni's use of series of lists without commas to separate the items. What effect does this have on the reader? You might read this as a poem of self-definition along with Lucille Clifton's "the thirty eighth year of my life."

Lucille Clifton, "the thirty eighth year of my life"

You might ask students to write a short prose piece or poem about the age they are now, an exercise in taking stock, which is in some sense what Clifton's poem is. What were the speaker's expectations for herself? What does she mean by "ordinary woman"? You could ask students to describe the actual life she probably lives. Much of the poem concerns the speaker coming to terms with her memories of her mother, who died in early middle age, not much older than the speaker is now. Is the speaker's loneliness in part grief for her mother? One discussion question might concern the tone of the poem: do students think the speaker is happy or unhappy about her life? Ask them to cite evidence for each side. Clifton's poem compares well with Janice Mirikitani's "Breaking Tradition" in the section "Women and Men."

Adrienne Rich, "Transit"

"Transit" is from <u>A Wild Patience Has Taken Me This Far</u> (1981), the collection that followed Rich's groundbreaking <u>The Dream of a Common Language</u> (1978). The poems in <u>A Wild Patience. . .</u> explore the past —either Rich's personal past (her mother, grandmothers, sister) or a historical past (Ethel Rosenberg, Emily Dickinson, Susan B. Anthony, and others) and try to integrate that past with the speaker's present. "Transit" concerns two sisters close in age but separate in their lives, one physically healthy and the other crippled (perhaps with the arthritis that plagues Rich). The third stanza is a flash of memory to their youth, climbing a mountain, both of them healthy and strong. In the rest of the poem, the sister is a skier and the speaker watches her walk toward a slope, skis shouldered. Why choose skiing as an image rather than, say, swimming or horseback riding or dancing? Why does Rich use and repeat the word "haunt" in the last stanza? What is the effect of the speaker naming herself "the cripple" in the last lines? Like Schreiber's "diagnosis (4-10-86)," "Transit" is about how illness interrupts the orderly progression of life stages.

Sharon Olds, "The Language of the Brag"

Giving birth as an epic heroic act, in the tradition of American expansiveness, is the subject of Olds's witty female challenge to the American male brag tradition in poetry and in life. See the Ginsberg poem "America" (itself a challenge) and share with students the first couple of pages of Whitman's Song of Myself (not included here, unfortunately) to see how Olds has mimicked their characteristic line length. Beyond the wit is the actual gritty and indeed heroic experience of giving birth which Olds images in all its messy powerfulness. How are the images in the first stanza of the poem in contrast to the powerful female images in the remainder of the poem? See also Plath's Three Women and the following two poems, by Ostriker and Derricotte, for more on pregnancy, birth, and motherhood.

Alicia Ostriker, "Propaganda Poem: Maybe for Some Young Mamas"

This "propaganda" poem is addressed to young feminists who might be considering the freedom of not having children at all. Written from within the feminist movement to young women, Ostriker, certainly a feminist herself, argues against the proposition that childbirth and motherhood are simply a trap for women. The poem begins with a parenthetical stanza that sets the scene — a confrontation between the visiting poet reading a poem about her pregnancy and a classful of young women who react with contempt. The body of the poem then alternates between 1) addressing and describing the young women in their need for separateness and freedom and 2) describing what it is like to be a woman with a child — the power and the pleasure of that primal connection. The postscript admits that, yes, children do limit you and provides brilliantly vivid images of what raising a child is like. The overall argument of the visiting poet is that a child connects you to living and to female power. You might ask students to outline the development of the speaker's argument and also the implied position of the young women in the class. Depending on the age of your students and whether or not they have children, you should have some passionate supporters on either side of this debate. This poem first appeared in Ostriker's volume, The Mother/Child Papers (1980).

Toi Derricotte, "Transition"

"Transition" is a section of Derricotte's book of poems about childbirth, <u>Natural Birth</u> (1983). We inadvertently omitted the last page of this poem in the text (it was at the printer before we discovered our mistake) and so we include the remainder of the poem here:

> i felt myself rise up with all the dead, climb out of
> the tomb like christ, holy and wise, transfigured with
> the knowledge of the tomb inside my brain, holding the
> gold key to the dark stamped inside my genes, never to
> be forgotten. . .

it was time, it was really time. this baby would be
born. it would really happen. this wasn't just a
trick to leave me in hell forever. like all the other
babies, babies of women lined up in rooms along the halls,
semi-conscious, moaning, breathing, alone with or without
husbands, there was a natural end to it that i was going
to live to see! soon i would believe in something larger
than pain, a purpose and an end. i had lived through to
another mind, a total revolution of the stars, and had
come out on the other side!

one can only imagine the shifting of the universe, the
layers of shale and rock and sky torturing against each
other, the tension, the sudden letting go. the pivot of
one woman stuck in the socket, flesh and bones giving
way, the v-groin locked, vise thigh, and the sudden
release when everything comes to rest on new pillars,
where is the woman who left home one night at 10 p.m.
while everyone was watching the mitch miller xmas show?
lost to you, to herself, to everyone

they finished watching the news, went to sleep,
dreamed, woke up, pissed, brushed their teeth, ate
corn flakes, combed their hair, and on the way out
of the door, they got a phone call. . .

while they slept the whole universe had changed.

Transition is the intense stage of childbirth between active labor, which can go on for many hours, and delivery, which is usually fast. In

23

transition the cervix is fully dilated. For some women this stage is characterized by nausea, trembling of thighs and legs, chills and contractions close together. For other women contractions slow down in this stage, and they are able to rest. The latter seems to be the case for the woman giving birth in Derricotte's poem.

The opening image of "Transition," "the meat rolls up and moans on the damp table," picks up from the previous poem, "10:29," where she writes of the pain of labor: "my heart is frozen like a calf on ice. my heart is/empty meat. my heart, my love is frozen. i will never/love again."

In "Transition" the speaker of the poem observes her laboring self admiringly as though she were "some other woman." The "she" throughout this poem does not appear to be the actual coming child, but this self of hers which is being born as well as giving birth. How does the poem move from personal to universal images? How is this birthing an act of spiritual and physical wholeness? Compare the poem to Plath's and to Olds's descriptions of giving birth and to Ostriker's assessment of the meaning of giving birth.

William Carpenter, "Rain"

Like Forché's "The Colonel" and Griffin's "This is a Story of a Day in the Life of a Woman Trying," "Rain" is a prose poem and it is also a narrative poem. It tells a story, actually two stories, one —the fantasy about the rained on city — inside the framing story of (and inside) the middle-aged man standing in the rain. What does the man's age have to do with the events in the poem? Again, you might contrast "Rain" to Eliot's "Prufrock" and to Justice's "Men at Forty" as a mode of response to aging (especially from a male perspective). See "How Poetry Works" for some discussion of sound effects in the poem. "Rain" is the title poem of Carpenter's prize winning volume of narrative poems.

Judith Ortiz Cofer, "Old Women"

The two central stanzas of this poem image the "little packages" mentioned in the epigraph. What are the items these little packages consist of? What is happening to them; what are they becoming under those mattresses? You might ask students to discuss whether they see "Old Women" as a positive poem about old age or not. Compare the poem with other images of aging included here: in Freeman's "A

Mistaken Charity," Silko's "Lullaby," Beckett's "Krapp's Last Tape," and poems by Shakespeare, Klepfisz, Vivien, and Yeats in this section.

Pat Mora, "Immigrants"

Chicana poet Pat Mora was born in El Paso, Texas; "Immigrants" is from her second volume, <u>Borders</u>. Students who are <u>not</u> children of immigrants sometimes express annoyance at "people who come to this country and don't bother [<u>sic</u>] to learn English." Perhaps this poem can lead to a useful discussion about this. By the time we learn that immigrant parents in the poem "speak" English to their children but only "whisper" their native language to them, we no doubt have caught the poem's satiric attitude towards the mainstream American culture these parents are trying to carry their children into and have understood, a little better, the reasons an immigrant might have misgivings about the very difficult task of assimilation. Ask students what effect "that dark/parent fear" might have on a child growing up.

Simon J. Ortiz, "My Father's Song"

Simon J. Ortiz grew up on the Acoma Reservation in New Mexico. He studied writing at the University of Iowa and has taught at the University of New Mexico and elsewhere. Since he moved, in a sense, out of one culture and into another, his childhood memories, like those of the poem's speaker, are no doubt very dear to him. In the poem, what the father has said is called "song" because of "the tremble of emotion" in it and because of its current importance to the speaker. Probably a writer, the speaker is struggling to find the right words, "Wanting to say things." In his memory of the discovery of the baby mice, his father, too, was "saying things," yet the speaker never mentions a single thing his father said. For it was his father's kind act — saving the mice — that did all the saying.

Ron Schreiber, "diagnosis (4-10-86)"

The diagnosis, of course, is AIDS. This is the first poem in <u>John</u>, Schreiber's volume of poetry about his lover. The speaker is "stunned" by the diagnosis, by the way everything is suddenly changed. First he is angry at the unfairness of it ("what about co-/factors!"; "what about the incubation/period!"); then he tries to tell himself he's lucky ("more than most people get"). Finally he can't help but see, in the death sentence the younger man faces, that his future has been cut off too, that the kind of happiness he's experienced with John "won't happen/to me again." You might ask students if they know someone who has, or had, AIDS.

DRAMA

Sylvia Plath, "Three Women"

Plath wrote this radio play in verse for the BBC in the spring of 1962. It is loosely based on a 1958 Ingmar Bergman film, Nara Livet (The Brink of Life or So Close to Life). The differences and similarities are suggestive. In Bergman's film the three women are Cecilia, a secretary who miscarries in her third month; Stina, a 25 year old factory worker who is married and wants to have her child, only to have it born dead; and Hjordis, a 19 year old factory worker who is not married, and comes to the hospital for an abortion, but changes her mind as a result of interactions with the other two women. In Bergman's film the three women develop a relationship with each other; in Plath's play they remain isolated from each other, though we readers see them in relation because Plath intercuts the monologues.

Concerning Plath's life — in the two years previous to writing "Three Women," Plath had had a miscarriage in hospital as well as giving birth to her two children, at home, with the help of midwives. Plath's positive experiences around pregnancy and birth happened away from hospital; her negative experience occurred in a hospital with the usual male attendance. (See the birth scene in Plath's novel The Bell Jar.)

There have been very few pieces of literature written about childbirth until recently, and students might discuss why that is so. We have included poems in this section by Olds, Derricotte, and Ostriker which students could read along with Three Women. You might also read "Three Women" along with the "baby factory" section of Huxley's Brave New World included in this section.

What kind of social comment is Plath making in "Three Women" about the possibilities for creativity in the modern world? Our own sense is that the Second Voice, the Secretary, is finally the defining and central experience in this play. She has more lines than the other two and she has the last word.

William Shakespeare,
The Tragedy of King Lear

We chose to include King Lear in the anthology rather than the more usual choices of Shakespeare plays — Hamlet, Macbeth, A Midsummer Night's Dream, The Tempest, Othello — partly because King Lear isn't taught enough at the introductory level. Yet it is really no more difficult than many other Shakespeare plays (or just as difficult, depending on your point of view). We also wanted to avoid a repetition of a play students might have read in high school. In addition, we felt that King Lear is one of the most moving and intelligent explorations in drama of the issues of aging and power.

Lear decides that he wants to retire, "to shake all cares and business from our age," and will divide his kingdom among his three daughters. Yet in his decision to give up political power, he is unable to let go of another kind of power. He insists that his daughters each convince him of the extent of their love for him; he will accordingly divide his kingdom in proportion to their love: "which of you shall we say doth love us most,/That we our largest bounty may extend/Where nature doth with merit challenge." Only trouble can come of this. It seems that Lear is trying to hold on to his power at the same time that he is ostensibly giving it up. Goneril and Regan go along with the game in self interest, but Cordelia, the youngest, possessed of some integrity, refuses to play. Students might be interested to consider how this plot line is based on folk or fairy tales in which it is often the youngest daughter who possesses goodness, is underrated, and triumphs in the end.

You might also consider King Lear in conjunction with Antigone (in "Varieties of Protest") in terms of the youth vs. age issue in that play and in terms of power conflicts. In Antigone, King Creon is trying to maintain his power in the face of Antigone's integrity, her need to act as her conscience tells her to, rather as Cordelia is here. Lear, by dividing his kingdom up before he dies and on such specious grounds, causes the very political catastrophe he had hoped his early retirement would avert — "that future strife/May be prevented now." This could be a question for discussion: do students think Lear's method of deciding how to divide his kingdom causes the plotting, the greed, the deaths that follow or, given the character of Goneril and Regan (and their husbands), would it all have happened anyway no matter how gracefully and honestly Lear had relinquished power?

As is often the case in both classical Greek and in Shakespearean drama, much plot action and resulting tragedy arise out of misunderstanding as well as misuse of power. Lear, blinded by his need to maintain power over his daughters by bribing them for their love, cannot see into their characters, cannot see until too late, when he really is blind, that Cordelia is the one who does care for him as a daughter.

The subplot of Gloucester and his two sons provides a parallel to Lear and his daughters and the subplot centering on the Fool provides satiric commentary on the main plot and allows for Lear's growth into tragic awareness of his mistake.

We find that focusing on the human issues that are powerfully present in Shakespearean drama — in <u>King Lear</u> aging, political power, and family dynamics — rather than focusing on the often confusing details of early 17th century stage conventions and language is a more rewarding approach for students in introductory literature classes.

Samuel Beckett, <u>Krapp's Last Tape</u>

This play might be a good choice with which to begin students' study of drama, since it is short, a one-act play, has only one character (even though mirrored in his tapes) and one setting. With drama, it is usually a good idea to ask students to consider staging, lighting, and other visual elements. Ask students to write briefly about or get a discussion going about what we learn about Krapp even before he says a word. From the way Beckett dresses him, from the setting he's given, what can we guess about this man? Then the first long paragraph gives us further information. From the way Krapp moves, from his relation to his setting and from what he does in that minute before he speaks, what can we infer about who Krapp is?

Once into the play, students might consider (or list) both what is comic and what is pathetic about Krapp (and what is both comic and pathetic at the same time). In terms of our human response to this character, do we find him likable?

Krapp continuously consumes bananas on stage and at frequent intervals goes offstage to drink. We could say he's a habitual user of bananas and alcohol, and his tapes from 30 years previous indicate he was then too. To what extent is Krapp's listening to his tapes also an addiction? To what extent do they keep him from living his life in the present? What is his life in the present anyway?

Ask students to discuss the scene in the punt Krapp's earlier self describes. Why does the older Krapp keep going back to that scene and that passage? Perhaps it's not only the scene and the meaning evoked but the language, the simple eloquence with which it is told. An excellent choice to read along with <u>Krapp's Last Tape</u> is Eliot's "The Love Song of J. Alfred Prufrock." Compare Krapp's moment in the punt with the moment which Prufrock lets pass him by, in the stanza that ends "in short, I was afraid." Students generally enjoy comparing Krapp and Prufrock, their sense of themselves, their attitude toward age, their personalities (which one would you most enjoy spending an hour chatting with?), their worlds (or settings) and their relation to them.

Finally, ask students to consider the last words of the play (spoken by the Tape, not by the present Krapp) — that he wouldn't want those years back.

NONFICTION

Maxine Hong Kingston, "No Name Woman"

"No Name Woman" is the first of five sections or chapters (all of which work as separate "stories") of Kingston's first book, The Woman Warrior: Memoirs of a Girlhood Among Ghosts (1976). Though this book won the National Book Critics Circle award for the best book of nonfiction published that year, The Woman Warrior lives on the border between fiction and nonfiction and so definitions of genre can be usefully discussed here. Ask students what they see as elements of nonfiction and of fiction or story-telling. The narrator makes up at least four different stories to account for her aunt, in the paragraphs that begin: 1) "perhaps she encountered him. . ."; 2) "The work of preservation demands. . . "; 3) "It could very well have been, however.. . "; and 4) "He may have been somebody in her own household. . ." The narrator's mother has given her "the facts," the story of the adultery, pregnancy and community punishment; the narrator tries to give her aunt a history and a personality. How does this act of creation connect to the title and to her statement in the concluding paragraph — "I alone devote pages of paper to her" — even though she tells us she has not pressed her mother for more "facts." What is the tension going on in this story for the narrator between fact and fiction, fact and imagination?

What do we do with the stories we've been told in our own lives? What ghosts do we each have to cope with? Her mother is using this story as a teaching device; what is the daughter doing with it? And what is her mother trying to teach her? Also, note another level of "fiction" versus "nonfiction" — how the narrator moves back and forth between her own autobiography and the fantasies about her aunt.

"No Name Woman" may be compared/contrasted with the excerpt from Audre Lorde's Zami. Students might also read Kincaid's "Girl" and the section from Edmund White's A Boy's Own Story.

Audre Lorde, from <u>Zami: A New Spelling of My Name</u>

Lorde calls this autobiographical book a biomythography, which suggests that she, like Kingston, is playing with the boundaries between fact and fiction. However, whereas Kingston plays with those boundaries in formal ways in "No Name Woman," Lorde tells this story of a Barbadian/American girl's arrival at puberty in a fairly straightforward linear narrative. Other comparisons students might explore are around the relationship between mother and daughter in each story. Though the mother in <u>Zami</u> is sometimes distant and harsh, there seems to be less struggle here at a fundamental level than there is in the Kingston piece. The relation there between the narrator and her mother's culture is problematic and scary and the narrator resists and transforms the "materials" her mother gives her to work with. In <u>Zami</u>, the Barbadian mortar and pestle are representative for the girl of her mother's culture. And both mortar and pestle are described in vivid, sensual and loving language. You could discuss why Lorde gives us the description of pounding seasoning for souse before she plunges into the story of her first menstruation. What does she gain by doing that? That opening passage ends with "The last day I ever pounded seasoning for souse. . . " Why doesn't she ever pound seasoning for souse again? Does it mark and become symbolic of the end of childhood in a deflected, and therefore easier to cope with, way than the actual fact of menstruation? Compare the first and second spice pounding — how do the metaphor of the mortar and pestle and the actual act of pounding the spice become transformed, internalized, connected with the body? You can use this section from <u>Zami</u> to demonstrate how a central metaphor can structure a piece of prose. In Kingston's "No Name Woman," in contrast, we have a story inside the main story providing that central organizing function.

WOMEN AND MEN

The selections in this section are so various and rich with possibility that you will undoubtedly come up with combinations and pairings of texts that we haven't thought of. However, here are some ideas that we have used. The Chopin, Gilman, Lawrence, Hemingway, and Mason stories; the Ibsen and Glaspell plays; Hughes's poem "The Lovepet" and perhaps also Sexton's "For My Lover, Returning to his Wife" all focus on the tensions, hostilities, and sometimes violence of the power politics of love and marriage. The way men see women is the subject of Toomer's "Fern," Glaspell's play "Trifles," Baraka's "Beautiful Black Women" and, more indirectly, Shapiro's "Buick" and Erdrich's "Jacklight"; this theme is also a factor in Updike's "A & P" and, in a layered fashion, in Grahn's "Boys at the Rodeo." The way women see men is a theme in "Boys at the Rodeo," in Naylor's "Etta Mae Johnson," and in Brady's "I Want a Wife." A point to discuss perhaps is why there are fewer examples of the way women see men than the way men see women. The question of gender identity and social roles — what it means to be a man; what it means to be a woman —is a crucial aspect of the Hemingway, Updike, Mason, and Yamauchi stories; and of poems by Broumas, Mirikitani, Cofer, and Rushin. This theme also comes up in the Woolf, Truth, and Brady pieces in the nonfictional prose section. On the issue of love and romance, Donne, Blake, Millay, Plath, and Naylor have something to say. Same-sex relationships with family members, friends, or lovers are central to the excerpt from Plato's Symposium, Naylor's "Etta Mae Johnson," and poems by Lim, Broumas, and Bloch.

Also note that pieces in other sections of this anthology might work well in conjunction with the selections included here. For example, from the Varieties of Protest section, Antigone, "The Heat Death of the Universe," the Adrienne Rich and Marge Piercy poems, and the Peggy Seeger song can be additional resources for your reading about women and men.

A small warning. People have strong opinions and feelings, sometimes quite close to the surface, about many of the issues the literature in this sections brings up. One of us practically had a riot on her hands the first time she taught "Trifles" (actually Glaspell's short story version of the play, called "A Jury of Her Peers"); the class immediately divided along gender lines and people started shouting at each other. There is a lot of energy available on the subject of women and men, which if you are wary and wily can be channeled into lively, even passionate, literary discussion and writing about literature. You might

want to start with a less volatile issue than the subject of "Trifles" —
which is killing a husband. Maybe you could begin instead with Donne's
comic "The Flea" or Bobbie Ann Mason's contemporary story about the
break up of a marriage, "Shiloh," or with Brady's satiric essay "I Want a
Wife." The Brady essay, for example, offers hard-hitting criticism but
somehow manages not to offend most people, perhaps because of the
humor.

FICTION

Charlotte Perkins Gilman, "The Yellow Wallpaper"

While "The Yellow Wallpaper" is Gilman's best known piece of writing, she wrote a great deal in addition to this story. Probably next best known, since it was brought back into print in the last decade, is her utopian feminist novel, Herland, about an all woman society stumbled on by three male explorers. Told from the point of view of the most balanced and "redeemable" of the three men, she explores in that novel a number of flaws in male/female relations and in institutionalized patriarchy. Herland, along with its two sequels, was first published serially in The Forerunner, a utopian socialist feminist journal that Gilman published and did practically all the writing for from 1909 to 1916. In it she also explored such issues as companionate marriage and family economics, suggesting such innovations as family apartment complexes that would have a common kitchen and housekeeping and child care techniques that would free women from the isolation and burden of domestic labor.

"The Yellow Wallpaper" was written some years earlier, while Gilman was still struggling with how to be a writer and a wife at the same time. (She ended her first marriage fairly quickly.) That struggle is central to the story and produces in the first person narrator, locked in an upstairs room "for her own good" and ordered not to write, an almost intolerable amount of stress. The question that invariably comes up in class discussion and so is a good way into the story is: 1) whether the narrator is indeed "crazy" by the end of the story, 2) whether she becomes crazy progressively through the story, or 3) whether she is already crazy when she begins to tell the story. What are our definitions of insanity and sanity? Is the narrator of "The Yellow Wallpaper" "mad" in one or both senses of that word (angry or crazy)? Here and in some other pieces like Adrienne Rich's poem "The Trees" and Pamela Zoline's story "The Heat Death of the Universe," the tension between breakdown and breakthrough is a useful way to discuss the trapped situation of the female protagonist.

D.H. Lawrence, "The White Stocking"

Many students will find this story quite disturbing, as they should. Their visceral reactions, especially to Ted's physical violence against Elsie, are perhaps the best place to begin. Though Lawrence presents marriage, and male-female relations generally, in terms of passion, connection, even transcendence, he also portrays them as power struggles. Ted has power over Elsie because she loves him, because he's husband (and breadwinner) not wife, and so on; Elsie has power over Ted because Sam Adams wants her, because she can hide, and reveal, Adams's gifts, because she loves Ted less than he loves her; finally, Ted, feeling threatened, losing control, resorts to the power his greater physical strength gives him. (And, of course, Adams's social class gives him power over both of them, and adds further tension to the relationship between Ted and Elsie.) Students will no doubt disagree about who or what's to blame for what happens between Ted and Elsie; they'll probably disagree even more on where they think Lawrence stands. You might ask them each to write in one sentence what they think Lawrence is trying to say in the story.

Ernest Hemingway, "The Short Happy Life of Francis Macomber"

This is a good story to use early on. It's lively, even exciting, and it's very accessible; students will not respond to it with silence. It also ends with a puzzle — did Margot Macomber kill her husband accidentally or deliberately? — and students should be encouraged to marshal evidence for whichever position they take. But the story is most valuable, in a course segment on "Women and Men," for the stark and dramatic way it raises important issues of sexual politics. Frances Macomber becomes a man (he "come[s] of age," as Wilson puts it) by hunting fearlessly; brave, cold, tight-lipped Wilson represents the standard of manhood against which Macomber is measured. But Macomber's achievement of manhood comes only in the last minutes of his life (hence the story's title). For most of the story he's a failure as a man; he's not a real man, in Hemingway's terms, just as Margot, with all her "bitchery" (as Macomber puts it), is not a real woman. Their marriage is a struggle for power (this story might be read with D.H. Lawrence's "The White Stocking") and the 'problem' with it all along is that the husband is not strong enough and the wife is not weak enough. A few men and many women students will probably get quite angry at this story; encourage them to spell out why. Any work of fiction embodies, and promotes, a set of values. "Macomber," because it so forcefully promotes such blatantly sexist values, will help students understand this and also understand that they can be "resisting readers" (to use Judith Fetterley's phrase), that they needn't passively accept the values of whatever 'great literature' they read. (You'll probably also want to raise the question of Hemingway's portrayal, and view, of Africa and Africans.)

Bobbie Ann Mason, "Shiloh"

Leroy and Norma Jean married too young, out of necessity not love, and, by never talking to each other about the death of their baby, ensured that they would grow apart not together over the years. Their names — he's "the king" and she's the future Marilyn Monroe — suggest very traditional sex roles, but their life, especially since Leroy's accident, reverses them: Leroy stays home, does needlepoint and macramé, daydreams; Norma Jean holds down a job, goes to night school to get ahead in the world, builds up her pectorals. But Norma Jean's decision to leave Leroy is, nonetheless, "one of those women's lib things." She may have little awareness of feminism, even consciously reject it, but her efforts to take charge of her own life, to free herself from a mother who still treats her like a child and a husband to whom she's a stranger, would have been much less likely, and much more difficult, without the changes brought about by "women's lib."

Students may miss some of the humor in "Shiloh." Mason certainly sympathizes with her characters, but she also keeps us at an often comic distance from them. When Norma Jean discusses her drugstore job with Leroy, explaining "the three stages of complexion care, involving creams, toners, and moisturizers," he "thinks happily of other petroleum products — axle grease, diesel fuel" and sees this as "a connection between him and Norma Jean." Mason, here, is not only suggesting how out of touch Leroy is with the emptiness of his marriage, but also — as she does throughout the story — suggesting how densely populated with the things of modern consumer society her characters' world is. While Norma Jean seems determined to make her own place within this world, Leroy is more passive and more alienated. (It's his perception that "subdivisions are spreading across western Kentucky like an oil slick.") Norma Jean is moving vigorously ahead, while Leroy is all

37

passivity (aided by his marijuana smoking) and stasis (the present tense narration highlights this) and nostalgia (his daydreaming, his plans to build a log cabin). Neither character's future holds tremendous promise (especially given the constraints their social class places on them), but it is Leroy who has suffered real defeat at Shiloh.

You might be surprised by the intensity of disagreement if you ask students whether Norma Jean <u>should</u> have left Leroy.

John Updike, "A & P"

The supermarket represents many things to Sammy. It represents conformity (the customers are "sheep," "houseslaves," "scared pigs in a chute"). It represents a dull future in a small town at a dead-end job, becoming like Stokesie ("married, with two babies") or like McMahon ("patting his mouth and looking after [Queenie and her friends] sizing up their joints," a sort of degenerated version of what Sammy now does) or, worst, like Lengel. It represents for a him a world of demanding, aging, unattractive, angry women (the cash-register-watching "witch," the women "with six children and varicose veins mapping their legs," the "young married screaming with her children" in the parking lot). The three "girls" who saunter in, on the other hand, represent youth, sexiness ("sweet can," "scoops of vanilla"), rebellion (they come in wearing bathing suits; they challenge Lengel), and a higher social class (those herring snacks and Queenie's voice). Their minds are pleasantly confusing ("just a little buzz like a bee in a glass jar") not nasty and calculating like that of the "witch" who catches Sammy ringing up her crackers twice. So when a conflict breaks out between the manager of the supermarket and the "girls," Sammy takes sides quickly and then acts, perhaps a bit too quickly. His chivalric gesture, his archetypal young man's attempt to impress the other sex, is inevitable, and probably self-destructive. "A & P" raises a number of interesting issues, especially the sexual politics of youthful efforts at asserting masculinity.

Judy Grahn, "The Boys at the Rodeo"

This story appeared in <u>True to Life Adventure Stories, Volume I</u>, an anthology Grahn edited of fiction mostly by working-class women. (There's also a second volume of true to life adventure stories.) Judy Grahn is known primarily as a poet. Her collection, <u>The Work of a</u>

Common Woman, includes her first five volumes of poetry and is named after The Common Woman Poems, a sequence of seven portraits of "ordinary" and representative women. "Ella, in a square apron, along Highway 80" is included in the "Money and Work" section. See also Grahn's long poem, "A Woman is Talking to Death," in "Varieties of Protest."

Grahn is a lesbian feminist writer, who established one of the first feminist small presses in the country in order to publish her own work and that of other lesbian feminist writers whose work was too radical for mainstream presses. The following remark is attributed to her: "Self publishing isn't vanity; it's an act of subversion." Gradually, and in spite of her politics, Grahn is beginning to be recognized by the literary establishment as a major voice in American poetry.

In "Boys at the Rodeo" she explores some of the implications of gender identification. The six adult women who go to the rodeo, because they are not dressed, or made up, or otherwise like feminine stereotypes, are taken for adolescent boys. This gives them the freedom of men for an afternoon and allows the narrator and the other five both to experience the event as insiders and to comment on the event from their perspective outside the assumptions the males at the rodeo accept unquestioningly. "We achieve the status of 14 year old boys, what a disguise for traveling through the world. I split into two pieces for the rest of the evening."

What are the components of the rodeo as a male ritual? Students might compare Grahn's "outside" perspective to the "inside" perspective of Hemingway in "The Short Happy of Francis Macomber" and Updike in "A & P."

An interesting writing exercise in the mode of Grahn here is to ask male students to take on a female persona and female students to take on a male persona and write a scene of part or all of a typical day from that perspective. This can lead to energetic class discussion.

Wakako Yamauchi, "And the Soul Shall Dance"

There are several areas of ambiguity in this short story. The most central is the narrator's nine-year-old attitude toward Mrs. Oka, concentrated in the words "different" and "strange." As a child, the narrator can't really comprehend adult behavior anyway and, as a Japanese American, she doesn't have quite the same view of Mrs. Oka as do the Japanese adults in the community, for example the young truck driver: "Never, never, he said in wide-eyed wonder, had he seen a drunken Japanese woman." The narrator (in her nine year old persona) doesn't judge Mrs. Oka but simply presents the fragments she sees.

A formal ambiguity is in the two-tiered narration itself; the narrator is throughout the story nine years old but, we are told at the beginning, the narrator is, at the time of telling, now fifty years old and remembering this. At the end of the story, when she says, "I suppose. . . ," we seem to return to the adult narrator.

The narrator's attitude toward the events is ambiguous (and maybe ambivalent as well), in her only being able to tell the story now that "most of the principals are dead." There is some worry about betrayal here which writers often have to struggle with when using material from their own lives and which is probably compounded when one comes from subculture in American society — immigrant, black, working class, whatever. You could ask students to imagine writing (or even begin to write) a scene based on some disturbing event from their childhood and discuss how that feels, in the sense of breaking some unwritten code of secrecy. How would the people written about (family members, for example) feel about being written about?

Finally, there is a lovely emotional and lyrical ambiguity in the scene in the desert that gives the story its name. The narrator inadvertently spies on the intoxicated Mrs. Oka, gathering flowers and dancing in the desert, acting like adults are not supposed to act, "with childlike delight." It makes the narrator "stir with discomfort." What about the scene and Mrs. Oka in general would be so powerful that someone would write about it 40 years later?

Kate Chopin, "The Story of an Hour"

An example of the surprise ending short story associated with de Maupassant and O. Henry and developed around the end of the nineteenth century, "The Story of An Hour" not only surprises the reader but the surprise kills the main character, Louise Mallard. In the beginning of this short (approximately 1000 words) story, the protagonist learns of the death of her husband; at the end of the story he walks in the front door and she dies from the shock. In between these two dramatic events occurs the real action of the story, Louise Mallard's coming to self. After her initial grief, she goes alone to her room, sits exhausted, and gazes out the window. Then she realizes she is free and from now on can live for herself. "There would be no powerful will bending her in that blind persistence with which men and women believe they have a right to impose a private will upon a fellow creature." You could ask students to discuss this statement as a definition of love and/or marriage. Finally, for Louise, love counts little next to assertion of self. Having come to this realization, which negates a great deal in her training as a female and her life as a married woman, how could she possibly go back to her previous protective blindness. Chopin has Louise die of shock (having initially given her a heart condition). If Louise had lived, how would she have coped with the knowledge she now possesses? Chopin's best known work, her novel <u>The Awakening</u> (1900), is the story of a woman, Edna Pontillier, who essentially does come to Louise Mallard's awareness while she, Edna, is still married. Edna tries in a variety of ways to free her body, mind, and soul; she ends, however, by drowning herself.

Jean Toomer, "Fern"

<u>Cane</u>, a major work of the Harlem Renaissance, is not a novel but a connected collection or sequence of sketches, short stories, poems, and a play. Roughly divided into three parts, the first section, which includes "Fern," is set in the south and deals with both the pain and beauty of the south from the perspective of a black man. The second section, set in the north, explores the vitality and constrictions of urban northern black life. In the third section, a northern black man (a school teacher) returns to the south and tries to make some connection to his ambivalent American heritage. Toomer himself was clearly ambivalent about his identity. Though considered one of the greatest writers of the Harlem Renaissance, Toomer's light skin gave him the choice of crossing the color line and he did, as one literary historian put it, finally decide to pass into white obscurity.

Here, Fern represents for the male narrator much more than who she is as a person. What are Fern's characteristics that are important to the narrator? What does he choose to say about her, from sexuality to spirituality? One major aspect of her image for him is her self-sufficiency. He can't possess her; nor can any man. He says, "As you know, men are apt to idolize or fear that which they cannot understand, especially if it be a woman." How come? And do women do the same to men? If the class decides that women are indeed more mysterious to men than men are to women, why might that be so?

Students might compare "Fern" to Claude McKay's "The Harlem Dancer," André Breton's "Freedom of Love", Amiri Baraka's "Beautiful Black Women," and Karl Shapiro's "Buick."

Gloria Naylor, "Etta Mae Johnson"

Mattie seems to have accepted her lot, finding her solace in the church. But not Etta. She refused to accept the limitations society put on someone born poor, black, and female. She fought off a sexual attack by a white man, fled to save her life, and kept moving. She refused to accept poverty, she ignored the disapproval of those who thought her disreputable, and she played the game as coolly as a man. But she is getting older and she is tiring of all the maneuvering (hence the "freedom she found in Mattie's presence [where] she had no choice but to be herself"). Tough as she is, Etta remains, at some level, naive and romantic, protecting a part of herself from the cold calculating her world demands —how else can we explain her falling for the transparent Reverend Woods, her belief that he'd actually marry her? When her head clears, and she sees him for what he is, she returns to Mattie, to "the love and the comfort that awaited her." (Is the story saying that admirable as Etta may be for refusing to accept her 'place,' she's playing a losing game?) What counts is the love of a good friend. Their shared past, their mutual understanding as women, their rich humor bind Etta and Mattie together while, as Etta herself says at one point, "All the good men are either dead or waiting to be born." One approach to teaching this story is, again, to play devil's advocate. Etta and Reverend Woods are experienced, consenting adults. Why is he portrayed as the villain, the one who's used her ? Doesn't Etta get what she deserves? In opposing this interpretation (which at least some are bound to do), students will need to discuss the ways in which the whole sexist social framework guarantees that the encounter between Etta and Reverend Woods is not an encounter of equals. This story might be read along with the two samples in this section of what Mattie calls "loose-life music": "How Much Can I Stand?" by Gladys Bentley and "Down Hearted Blues" by Alberta Hunter and Lovie Austin.

POETRY

John Donne, "The Flea"

As with most poems, it is helpful first to have students figure out what literally is happening in this poem. Then, since this is a clever and opportunistic seduction argument, what are the stages of the argument and how does the speaker of the poem use the (implied) events to advance his cause? The speaker uses humor as well as logic and emotional appeal and you could ask students to point out examples of all three of these modes. Though only one person is speaking, how does the poet manage to conjure up for us quite vividly the second person?

You could ask students to compare this poem to another, and as famous, carpe diem poem, Marvell's "To His Coy Mistress" — in tone, use of imagery, method of argument. How effective do students think each is in achieving its goal?

You might also compare "The Flea" with the other two Donne poems in this section — "The Sun Rising" and "The Canonization," again in tone, use of imagery, and method of argument.

William Blake, "The Garden of Love"

Blake contrasts nature, joy, spontaneity, affirmation with punishing denial and with death —both of which he associates with organized religion. Socialization into adulthood destroys childhood innocence and pleasure; the growth of institutionalized religion has made society repressive. For Blake the anarchist and celebrator of sexuality (see his "Proverbs of Hell"), "binding with briars my joys and desires" is the worst sin imaginable. The rhythm and the internal rhyme of the last two lines dramatize the repression and regimentation that religion has brought to the Garden ("priests are patrolling the area," as one student put it). This poem should provoke considerable discussion.

Edna St. Vincent Millay, "Love is not all: it is not meat nor drink"

See the brief comment on this sonnet in "How Poetry Works." Worth discussing are the irony and indirectness of this love poem in contrast to poems like Donne's "The Canonization," and Elizabeth Barrett Browning's "How Do I Love Thee?" The mode here is finally to profess love but to get there through negatives. Perhaps Millay takes this approach because she is writing in a less clearly romantic and more ironic age, an age that doesn't see love either as eternal or as unaffected by material conditions. What are the material conditions Millay suggests that, not only in her own case but in general, might affect whether love can survive — food, shelter, health, etc.? Also, what part does choice about loving play in this poem?

Anne Sexton, "For My Lover, Returning to His Wife"

If we separately list the images associated with the wife ("she") and those associated with the husband's lover ("I"), a fairly clear contrast emerges. His wife represents security, stability, children; she was made for him (first stanza); she takes care of his everyday needs ("sees to oars and oarlocks for the dinghy"); she's "solid," a "monument"; etc. His lover, on the other hand, embodies excitement, adventure, the exotic ("A bright red sloop," "Littleneck clams out of season," and so on). In her own life, the wife has security and stability (unless he leaves her), but no adventure, it seems; his lover has adventure (provided another man comes along), but lacks security, stability, children. But the man can have it all. This observation can be the starting point for an important discussion of sexual politics. You might ask students to speculate on the source and extent of each partner's power and freedom in the two relationships described in the poem.

Genny Lim, "Wonder Woman"

One tendency in the Women's Movement (a tendency often identified with "radical feminism") has been to view sexism as the central form of social oppression and patriarchy as the model for and cause of other forms of social inequality. Thus all women are united as victims of sexist attitudes, individuals, and institutions. Some feminists — often Third World women — have had problems with this view: 'if my mother's job was cleaning your mother's kitchen floor, are we really united in our oppression as women?' The speaker in the poem is trying to come to grips with these issues. She sees the contradictions ("copper-tanned women in Hyannis Port playing tennis" and "women in factories punching time clocks"), yet she clings to a vision of all women united. A (presumably) middle-class, Asian-American woman, she wants, despite the difficulties, to identify with the struggle and the dreams of "women along the Mekong."

Amiri Baraka, "Beautiful Black Women"

Like many other movements, the movement for black power and black liberation in the 1960s, especially later in the decade and especially in the urban North, was dominated by men. Before black feminism developed and grew, male leaders often defined the movement's aim as reclaiming 'our manhood' — which, of course, rendered black women invisible, their role being to work back stage to support men. If challenged, men argued that things were so bad (and, of course, they were very bad indeed) that black people couldn't yet afford to deal with issues of sexism, which would only divide and weaken them in the fight against racism. The speaker in the poem, choosing to speak for black men ("we"), wants black women to "Help us get back what was always ours." As helpers, the "Beautiful black women" are loved, even placed on a pedestal ("you, reigning, black queen"), but clearly subordinated.

Karl Shapiro, "Buick"

A picture of an early 1950s Buick, if you can find one, should help students understand the physical details ("hips of a girl," "silvery nose," etc.) in the second stanza. Students who have cars probably love them and the class will no doubt have much to say in general about connections between cars and sex (whether in advertising or in life). But it's worth focusing the discussion on the male persona in this particular poem, who views his car as a woman and experiences love, lust, even jealousy (third stanza) as he drives. The poem, of course, says more about male attitudes towards women than towards cars and it provides an excellent opportunity to discuss 'objectification' of women.

Ted Hughes, "The Lovepet"

See the brief comment on "The Lovepet" in "How Poetry Works." This personification of married love as a viciously, voraciously hungry animal is in intense contrast to poems like Donne's "The Canonization," the "Song of Solomon" from the Old Testament, and Amy Lowell's "A Decade." On the other hand, students might compare "The Lovepet" to other poems that question romantic and satisfied love, like Anne Sexton's "For My Lover, Returning to His Wife," the two blues songs — "Down Hearted Blues" and "How Much Can I Stand?" — and Gregory Corso's poem "Marriage." The lovepet is neither the man or the woman, but the relationship itself, larger than the sum of its parts and out of control. People might want to think about (though they might not want to talk about) relationships in their own lives where they felt some fraction of the wholesale destruction in this poem begin to happen. How can personifying, imaging, metaphorizing the relationship in this way be more effective than straightforward telling of how a love relationship went bad?

Olga Broumas, "Cinderella"

"Cinderella" is from Broumas's first volume of poetry, <u>Beginning With O</u>, which won the Yale Younger Poets Award in 1977. Broumas has several reworked fairy tales in one section of that volume and students might wish to compare what Broumas does with the Cinderella tale to a couple of the actual fairy tale versions. A major change Broumas makes here is Cinderella's relation with her sisters, in the fairy tale her oppressors along with the ever present fairy tale ogre of a stepmother. Broumas seems to be viewing that as a motif used by men to divide and isolate women. Here the modern Cinderella superimposed on the fairy tale Cinderella is any token woman and, from a poet's perspective in particular, the successful woman writer, let into the male literary establishment as her remarks about language— "cracking the royal code" and "praise me my nimble tongue"—suggest. What does the speaker mean when she says, "I am a woman in a state of siege, alone..."?

Louise Erdrich, "Jacklight"

The doubleness suggested by a reading of this poem's epigraph (flirting/hunting; rape/bear killing) is paralleled in the situation the poem presents. As the footnote tells us, to jacklight is to flash a blinding light in the eyes of the hunted animal. But a jacklight is also a natural phenomenon, a flash of light in the dark due to mysterious natural causes. The poem is from the point of view of the deer who speak as "we". Pulled out of hiding by the mechanical lights the hunters have set up and are hiding behind, guns cocked, the deer pause at the edge of the woods. The first three stanzas of the poem describe the effect the light has on them, this invasion, this rape, of their darkness. Stanzas four, five, and six describe the hunters from the hunted animals' perspective. The sense used is primarily smell and the images are quite striking, almost surrealistic. You might ask students to analyze how each image and the collection of images of the hunters contribute to a particular tone and what that tone is. Stanza seven repeats much of the opening stanza but ends on a decision. The last stanza turns the narrative as the hunters become mesmerized by the jacklights flashing in the deep woods, put down their equipment, and step into the dark.

Christopher Marlowe, "The Passionate Shepherd to His Love"

A sixteenth century pastoral poem that paints a rustic and peaceful picture of romantic love, with flowers and birds and the sound of water-pebbled streams and pretty clothes and singing and dancing. A life, as the speaker suggests (since he twice uses the word) entirely composed of "pleasures." As an argument, though perhaps more serious than simply seduction, it is similar to Donne's "The Flea" and Marvell's "To His Coy Mistress" — though more long term than carpe diem. For a humorous contemporary contrast, put this next to Gregory Corso's "Marriage" and also C. Day Lewis's "Come, live with me and be my love."

William Shakespeare, "When my love swears that she is made of truth"

Once it is clear that students understand the poem, line by line — including puns like "lie" and "vainly" — you might ask them to characterize the speaker, his beloved, and their relationship. What's the basis of their attraction to each other? What comes between them? A central question is the tone of the poem. Is the speaker content with playing the game he and his beloved are playing? And what do students think of all this? The poem could obviously open up a long discussion about 'relationships.'

Anonymous, "Song of Solomon"

A short excerpt from "The Song of Songs" in the Old Testament, King James version. We selected a representative piece, but students might enjoy reading this early love poem in its entirety. This part of the poem is mostly from the perspective of the man, except for verses 8 and 16, which are from the woman's point of view. Notice the use throughout of simile and metaphor — compare to André Breton's "Freedom of Love" and Christina Rossetti's "A Birthday" (the latter included in "How Poetry Works"). Notice also the sensuousness of much of the imagery. You could discuss the concluding and perhaps controlling metaphor of the garden in verses 12 - 16.

John Donne, "The Sun Rising"

See the brief comment on "The Sun Rising" in "How Poetry Works." We chose to include this poem, "The Canonization," and others with modern spelling, but you might want also to show students a copy of the originals, to give the 17th century flavor. It is useful as always to begin with a discussion of what is literally happening in the poem, then to move on to the poem's argument, here addressed by the speaker of the poem to the personified sun. How does the poet characterize the sun and how is that in aid of his argument? How does the speaker characterize love? Compare this poem, in method of argument, with Donne's "The Flea".

John Donne, "The Canonization"

Ask students to look up "canonize" or "canonization." In the last stanza Donne refers to "reverend love". How is Donne characterizing love in this poem? You might usefully compare/contrast it to the other two Donne poems in this section. Students could speculate on who the "you" is that the poem is addressed to. And more obviously, who the "you" is that is invoked in the final stanza by the more general you. What is the speaker's purpose? Why is he "speaking" the argument of this poem?

Andrew Marvell, "To His Coy Mistress"

This much taught and often analyzed poem is structured as a three-part argument, and you might begin by asking students to compare the three parts —in terms of tone, imagery, syntax, rhythm, etc. To begin discussing the sexual politics of the poem, you might ask students how persuasive the speaker's argument is, or even have them write a prose reply from the coy mistress. It might be useful to compare what the speaker says time will destroy in him with what he says it will destroy in her, and also ask what attitudes are revealed in lines 27-29. And, as with many works in this section, you might throw some light on gender roles by reversing them, that is, by asking how a poem, "To Her Coy Master," with a female speaker, would need to be different. "To His Coy Mistress" might be taught alongside Marlowe's "The Passionate Shepherd to His Love."

Elizabeth Barrett Browning, "How do I love thee?"

This sonnet, #43 of the 44 <u>Sonnets from the Portuguese</u>, may, due to imitation and excessive quotation, seem almost Hallmark Card-like to students. But a close reading should help them get past this. You might ask students to characterize as precisely as possible each kind of love the speaker counts. You might also mention that Browning has chosen a form— the cycle of love sonnets — traditionally used by men and ask whether, if we did not know its author, we would be able to tell that this sonnet was written by a woman.

Walt Whitman, "To a Stranger" and "I Saw in Louisiana a Live-Oak Growing"

These are two poems of passion and loneliness. In the second, the speaker can think of "little else" than of his "own dear friends," yet he is alone, and starts out identifying with a solitary tree. In the first, he looks "longingly" at a stranger, feels intensely connected to this stranger, yet does not speak to him/her. Given Whitman's life, the reference to "manly love," and what seems almost like an unwillingness on the speaker's part to identify the sex of the "stranger," it is important to relate the speaker's feelings to the poet's sexual orientation and the homophobia of the society he lived in. These two poems might be read along with Jack Anderson's "A Lecture on Avant Garde Art."

Emily Dickinson, "My Life had stood — a Loaded Gun"

This complex and difficult poem has been interpreted in many different ways, but in the context of other literary works about "Women and Men" students are likely to see in it — as Adrienne Rich does — a deep "ambivalence toward power." (See "Vesuvius at Home: The Power of Emily Dickinson," in Rich's book <u>On Lies, Secrets, and Silence</u>.) The speaker (presumably female) gains power through subservience to an "Owner" ("Him") — a power which is exhilarating but also dangerous.

Does the poem argue for the pursuit of such power (as a woman, as a poet)? Against it? Against subservience as an avenue to (perhaps illusory) power?

Amy Lowell, "A Decade"

Amy Lowell was an important poet in and organizer of the Imagist Movement (see brief discussion of Imagism in "How Poetry Works"). "A Decade" is built around two images that capture both the difference and the continuity in a relationship as it moves from initial romantic and passionate fervor — red wine, honey, burnt and sweet — with the satisfying morning bread taste and nourishment of a good healthy long term relationship. Lowell was perhaps writing this poem, as she did many of her love poems, to the woman she lived with. See also Alice Bloch's poem "Six Years" about a lesbian relationship that is becoming long term.

Alberta Hunter and Lovie Austin, song: "Down Hearted Blues"

Except for the first four lines (and this may be a variant in transcription) this song follows the classic blues pattern: the first line essentially repeated, with perhaps slight rephrasing, in the second line, with the third line providing the second half of the proposition or sometimes a resolution to the problem set up in the first two lines. What is the problematic situation this song proposes and what does the speaker plan to do about it? What is her attitude toward the situation? One definition of the blues is: a good man, or a good woman, feeling bad.

Claude McKay, "The Harlem Dancer"

This Harlem Renaissance sonnet evokes the night life of the 1920s in Harlem dance halls. Claude McKay's 1925 novel, <u>Home to Harlem</u>, about a young man returning home from World War I, captures in prose and in more detail the gaiety and vitality of Harlem night life during the period. It might be interesting, if you have a copy of that novel, to compare a prose description by McKay of a Harlem dance hall with this poem. There are three different perspectives in "The Harlem Dancer": the spectators', the speaker's, and (implied) the dancer's. You could ask students to compare/contrast them. A contemporary reference might occur to students: Tina Turner's "A Dancer For Money."

William Butler Yeats, "Leda and the Swan"

A detailed explanation of the Greek myth this sonnet is built around would probably be helpful in generating discussion, which might, among other things, touch on what the answer is to the last question in the poem. "Leda and the Swan" might also lead to a discussion of the sexual politics of myths — of myths, for example, in which the beauty of women (Leda, Helen) drives men (and male gods) to terrible acts, acts that lead to war and either individual or social destruction. This poem might be read with Muriel Rukeyser's "Waiting for Icarus."

Louise Bogan, "Women"

You could ask students to find a quality that fits each of Bogan's images of women. What do they think the speaker's tone is here? Does she simply dislike her own gender? Is she angry at/disgusted with herself and other women? Students might try to come up with: 1) a few images for men that would express certain qualities they think men possess; or 2) an alternate set of images for women that expresses their own sense of women. You could compare this poem to others written by American women poets at about the same time: the two blues songs, "How Much Can I Stand?" and "Down Hearted Blues," and Millay's "What Lips My Lips Have Kissed."

Gladys Bentley, song: "How Much Can I Stand?"

What's wrong with her current man? What do you think she means when she says: "the next man I get/must be guaranteed"? However, given the remainder of the concluding stanza, it doesn't sound like she has much optimism about him either. Compare with "Down Hearted Blues," also in this section. A good article about women's blues is Hazel Carby's "It Jus Bes Dat Way Sometime: The Sexual Politics of Women's Blues" in <u>Radical America,</u> vol. 20, no. 4.

André Breton, "Freedom of Love"

You might ask students, as an exercise in poetry writing, to pick a subject and imitate Breton's style: "My car with. . . "; "My friend with . . . "; "My dog with . . . "; etc. The temptation to parody will be great, but students will probably learn something about imagery. As for Breton's poem — the key question is how he views his wife. What patterns are there in his images? What is the significance of his <u>partitioning</u> his wife as he does? (How does it compare to what the speaker does in Marvell's "To His Coy Mistress"?) Students might be invited to write Breton's speaker's wife's reply: "My husband with. . . " This poem could usefully be taught alongside "Buick" by Karl Shapiro.

Gwendolyn Brooks, "when you have forgotten sunday: the love story"

Clearly the speaker hasn't forgotten, for every detail is lovingly recreated. The poem is one long periodic sentence that sweeps the reader along; by the time the last line arrives, the "you" to whom this is addressed will certainly have had ample opportunity to begin remembering.

Owen Dodson, "Drunken Lover"

Most poems about lovemaking are celebratory; here's a contrast. It's hardly what was "dreamed" of in adolescence. Rather than an expression of love, it's something to "endure" for love.

53

Léopold Sédar Senghor, "You Held the Black Face"

Though at first glance simply a love poem, this is as well a poem of exile and homesickness. It might be useful to discuss the way the woman and the speaker's native land almost merge here. Is the woman primarily a metaphor for his homeland? Whatever, the images are gorgeous and worth studying line by line. Senghor, the best known Senegalese poet, wrote in French, and along with Aimé Césaire of Martinique and Léon Damas of French Guinea, became one of the apostles of the Negritude Movement in Paris in the 1930s. A khalam is a musical instrument.

Langston Hughes, "Mellow"

"Mellow" demonstrates the usual accessibility and deceptive simplicity of Hughes's poetry. "Mellow" is from Hughes's book-length sequence of poems, Montage of a Dream Deferred (see "Harlem" and "Ballad of the Landlord," also from that volume). Hughes based his poems often, and particularly in that volume, upon indigenous African-American music forms — jazz, blues, bebop, ragtime, boogie woogie, gospel. In this poem, you could ask students to discuss the apparent contradiction between the poem's title and the dangerous situation the poem portrays.

Gregory Corso, "Marriage"

What's pushing the speaker in the poem to marry? Why exactly is he resisting so strongly? (How does he undermine the traditional romantic images of courtship, wedding, honeymoon, married life?) Why his impulse to "take her. . . to cemeteries," act "the Mad Honeymooner," paste "Tannu Tuva postage stamps/all over the picket fence"?

Ask the class whether the speaker is just maladjusted, or if the problem lies outside him. The discussion is not so likely to break down along gender lines as it might have when this 1960 poem was first written.

Diane Wakoski, "Slicing Oranges for Jeremiah"

Wakoski is called a deep image poet, though her usual almost surrealistic juxtaposing of images is somewhat muted in this poem, except for such lines as "orange jelly, a goldfish/lights on the water at night." What do the oranges in the poem stand for? And what about the action of slicing oranges? What does the speaker of the poem say is the relation between women and men? How does she define or redefine strength and its consequences? What does she want for herself?

Nayo (Barbara Malcolm), "First Time I Was Sweet Sixteen"

Ask students what changes and what remains the same as the speaker moves from one relationship to the next. You might also ask them what advice they would give the speaker; have them write her a letter, perhaps. Be prepared to deal with any subtly or overtly racist responses to this poem; they could provide the occasion for an important discussion.

Marge Piercy, "The woman in the ordinary"

Boldly and directly, this poem dramatizes the contrast between personal potential and the limits of socially imposed gender roles. One way to approach it is simply to work through each image — "Christmas card virgin with glued hands," for example — and ask students to articulate precisely what they think Piercy is trying to suggest with it. Ask them also what Piercy achieves by juxtaposing such strikingly different images in the last two lines and whether the final image — which seems, after all, like the traditional image of woman as flower — in any way undercuts the impact of the rest of the poem, or whether Piercy is revising and reclaiming the flower image. The last five lines of this poem are discussed briefly in "How Poetry Works."

Adrienne Rich, "Trying to Talk with a Man"

We've included three Rich poems in this section (see "Diving Into the Wreck" and Poem XI of Twenty-One Love Poems), not only because Rich is one of the greatest living American poets, but because much of her best writing has been so centered on the intricacies of sexual politics between women and men and between women and women. The situation in this poem is of a man and a woman, probably married, who go to an anti bomb political protest, thinking they are united against a common enemy, and discover that there is a deeper layer or level of politics they now confront — sexual politics — not out there, but in here: in their relationship, in themselves.

Adrienne Rich, "Diving into the Wreck"

Here are some questions you might ask students to consider: What is "the book of myths"? And whom does the speaker mean when she says "our names do not appear" in it? Why does the poet make her persona a diver? What is she diving to and why? What are the "stages" of the dive? What does the speaker of the poem learn from/at each one? What does she mean when she says "the sea is another story?" Why is the title of the poem "Diving Into the Wreck" rather than "Diving Toward the Wreck." Some possible writing exercises: you might ask students to look up 'androgyny' and consider why the speaker of the poem says in stanza 8, "I am she: I am he." You might ask students to discuss their own experiences with swimming, snorkeling, or scuba diving, and the two different mediums of air and water. Explore the literal association of the poem's extended metaphor. Finally, the speaker of the poem says, "The words are purposes./The words are maps." Why does she talk about language here and what does this have to do with the overall metaphor of diving?

Muriel Rukeyser, "Looking at Each Other"

There are three other Rukeyser poems in the text students might look at to get a sense of the range of this poet: "Waiting for Icarus" in this section, "Waking This Morning" in Peace and War, and "Boy with His Hair Cut Short" in Money and Work. This poem demonstrates Rukeyser's strong sense of sensuality and the transcendent everydayness of passion. For Rukeyser, passion means more than the physical and erotic. In "Waking This Morning" she directly connects the ability to feel to her politics when she refers to the "anti-touch" people. Ask students to notice how she uses repetition here and in "Waiting for Icarus."

Muriel Rukeyser, "Waiting for Icarus"

See the discussion of this poem in "How Poetry Works." Ask students to look up the myth of Daedelus and Icarus (they may find more than one version) and to discuss the effectiveness for new insights and as a writing technique of taking on the perspective of a "minor" character in a historical or literary situation. Those minor characters are often women. You might discuss the effectiveness of repetition here and in the preceding poem, "Looking at Each Other."

Marge Piercy, "Barbie Doll"

This very accessible poem is good to use early on in a unit on "Women and Men." Just asking students to explicate "Barbie Doll" should open up a lively discussion on the ways we are socialized into traditional male and female roles. Her sex defines this "girlchild" (one word) from birth and the toys she is given prepare her to be mother, housewife, and lover. Despite her many good qualities, she is seen, and comes to see herself, as "a fat nose on thick legs." The advice she is given is contradictory ("coy," "hearty"), useless, in fact destructive, for it insists on locating the problem in her, not in those around her, or in society. Her final makeover is a success, for everyone calls her "pretty." Students may find the sarcasm too strong in Piercy's last stanza, but it is the natural conclusion to what comes before. Some may insist that there's just as much pressure on boys. You might outline a parallel poem, "Ken Doll," and ask if it would have the same impact. It would be interesting to teach "Barbie Doll" alongside the excerpt from Toni Morrison's The Bluest Eye in "Growing Up and Growing Older."

Jack Anderson, "A Lecture on Avant-Garde Art"

This poem opens up all sorts of questions for discussion. It covers repression, invisibility, and "triumphs." Students might be asked to expand on Anderson's claims that "on every side, images proclaim/and sustain the straight life" and that images of the gay life are "obscure," "kept locked." They might also be asked what they think the consequences of this might be, and what exactly they think Anderson means when he describes the gay life as "art." (And is there only one kind of "gay life"?) By "gay" Anderson seems to mean "gay male"; to what extent does what he says apply to lesbians? This poem might be read along with Plato's <u>Symposium</u>, the two Whitman poems, and "Boys at the Rodeo" in this section and also with the excerpt from <u>A Boy's Own Story</u> in the section "Growing Up and Growing Older."

ntozake shange, "With No Immediate Cause"

The speaker tries in a number of ways to convey the enormity of the problem of male violence and sexual abuse. She offers statistics ("every 3 minutes. . . "); she graphically describes specific acts ("held his old lady onto/a hot pressing iron"); she shares her own reaction to a world of men terrorizing women, as well as to the newspaper's concern that, "with no/immediate cause," women might strike back and hurt <u>men</u> ("I spit up i vomit i am screaming"). The speaker can't stomach the thought that the man she sits next to on the subway or casually buys the paper from might be committing such crimes. All men are potentially victimizers and all women, whether they have directly suffered attack or not, must live in fear ("we all have immediate cause") and therefore are already victims. Students will react strongly to this poem. Men will probably feel defensive and protest their own innocence; and some women may say that shange "exaggerates"; but out of the discussion there should at least emerge an understanding that women live with a whole set of concerns and fears that men do not share.

Adrienne Rich, Poem XI from <u>Twenty-One Love Poems</u>

See the discussion of this poem in "How Poetry Works." If you want to place the poem in context, the entire sequence of <u>Twenty-One Love Poems</u> is included in Rich's <u>Dream of a Common Language</u> (1978). The sequence is about a relationship between two women. Students can compare this poem to "Diving Into the Wreck," the title poem of the volume of Rich's poetry immediately preceding <u>Dream of a Common Language</u>. Contrast the "diving down" into water imagery to the climbing up the sides of a volcano (fire) imagery here and the androgyny in the earlier poem with the relationship between the two women in the second.

Janice Mirikitani, "Breaking Tradition"

See Lucille Clifton's "the thirty eighth year of my life" for another mother/daughter poem. Mirikitani is writing out of her Japanese cultural identity. The speaker of the poem, presumably a woman of middle years, is caught between the brash teenage Americanism of her daughter and the meek, kimono-wrapped silence she remembers of her Japanese mother. She denies she is like her mother; now her daughter denies she is like the woman who speaks this poem. What images does the poet use to characterize each of these three women? What images does she ascribe to women in general? What do the three women have in common in spite of their different lives? Or put another way, what are the similarities underlying the apparently disparate images of the three? To what extent are these women breaking tradition or not?

Marge Piercy, "Right to Life"

Who does "you" refer to in the second stanza? What, exactly, is Piercy saying in the third stanza? What does she achieve by changing <u>person</u> —"she," "you," "we," "I," — in the course of the poem? What meanings does the title hold?

Students are often quite passionate on the issue of abortion, so be prepared. You might try to focus the discussion by first asking students to rewrite Piercy's poem as a brief prose argument.

Jack Gilbert, "Love Poem"

What is the speaker's attitude toward the immigrant couple on the bus? Is he more sympathetic to the woman, or to the man, or do you see him as an impartial observer? Does his attitude change during the poem? What's going on between the couple? Why is the man embarrassed by the woman? Why does she persist in her enjoyment in spite of his resistance? "Knowing her role was to be wrong. She was wrong." The speaker of the poem seems to be looking at her in some sense through the eyes of the man, yet her unsophisticated joy finally takes over the poem. Why does Gilbert title it "Love Poem"? You could contrast this poem to Ted Hughes's "The Lovepet".

Alice Bloch, "Six Years"

In this poem, we learn almost as much about the speaker's lover as we do about the speaker herself. You might begin by asking students to characterize each woman as fully as possible and to try to explain why each one reacts the way she does to their being called "an old married couple." Early on, their differences were complementary; later they led to conflict; and now the lovers have become more alike, each taking on some of the other's better qualities. Their relationship is secure but not static; they're never quite sure how, but each day, one way or another, they come together: "We have no choice/of destination only the route/is a mystery." Their love is not "blessed" and it lives "in the space between the laws." So <u>are</u> they like a heterosexual married couple?

Martha Collins, "Several Things"

See the discussion of this poem in "How Poetry Works." We can see in the last stanza that the origin of the poem is a recipe. And this might be an occasion for students to consider where poems and stories start — from an incident, an image, a line, an observed character, an idea. You could ask students to each take a recipe they know of and imagine a situation from it that would turn into a poem or story. The poem here is playful; you get the sense of the poet's imagination creating the poem — several things could happen in this poem." The use of "could" and the use of questions offer possibilities and alternatives and provide the image of a mind at creative work. Who is the "you" who appears in the second to last stanza?

Judith Ortiz Cofer, "Claims"

See Cofer's other poem, "Old Women," in the Growing Up and Growing Older section. Also, see poems by Vivien and Klepfisz for positive images of women aging. You could ask students to consider the title of this poem, to think about what grandmother is claiming and also about what claims had been placed on her throughout her life. What was the pact she made with man and nature? What does saying it that way, combined with what she tells each of her daughters, suggest about her level of self knowledge? Ask students to trace the sea imagery in the poem and to analyze how Cofer uses that imagery to suggest more than one layer of meaning.

Kate Rushin, "Why I Like to Go Places: Flagstaff, Arizona — June 1978"

This poem and "The Black Back-Ups" (Money and Work) are included in Rushin's recently published first volume of poetry, The Black Back-Ups (1993). Students might want to look at the two poems together, noting how Rushin tells stories in her poems and how she uses repetition to create effective storytelling. This poem begins with restriction, with what this young woman (maybe a teenager) is not supposed to do: to go places, to go "off the block" and travel across the country the way an American male can do almost as an American rite of passage. The speaker of this poem does go, however, and meets George; and much of the rest of the poem is about the perhaps unlikely friendship she makes with George while avoiding the dire possibilities her mother and aunts predicted for this or any trip off the block. The speaker of the poem contrasts herself to writer Langston Hughes and his fictional character Jesse B. Simple. How is she supposed to learn about life so she can write about it if she's not allowed off the block? Students could look at this poem along with Woolf's "Shakespeare's Sister."

Barbara Kingsolver, "This House I Cannot Leave"

Rape is often used as a metaphor. And there certainly is a sense of violation when someone has broken in to the place where you live. The speaker's friend experiences it this way: the burglar "touched her clothes, passed through rooms/leaving himself there/staining the space." Friends don't quite understand how traumatic it was. The damage is greater than can be seen; the fruit trees have stopped growing "for her." If we haven't anticipated it, the word "me" near the end comes as a great shock. By then, we've begun to understand just how devastating this metaphoric rape was for the speaker's friend; how much worse, then, must the real thing be! This poem might be read alongside ntozake shange's "With No Immediate Cause."

Magdalena Gomez, "Chocolate Confessions"

What's wrong with the marriage in this poem? What problems does the speaker of the poem seem to be having? How does she propose solving them? How do food and body image intersect with the speaker's sense of her possibilities? You might ask students to imagine they are this woman's counselor, priest, or therapist. How would they describe her situation and what advice might they have for her? Can students empathize with any aspects of the situation depicted in this poem?

DRAMA

Henrik Ibsen, <u>A Doll's House</u>

"You have never loved me," Nora tells Helmer. "You only thought it amusing to be in love with me." This is as good a place as any to start a discussion of the nature of their relationship. What does this statement mean, exactly? How accurate is it? Is Helmer really that heartless? Nora is his "little bird," his "squirrel," his "lark," his "little featherbrain," and on and on — much, it might seem, to her delight, as she flutters around, merrily decorating the Christmas tree and flattering her husband's ego. To us today, no doubt, the problem with all this is sooner apparent than it was to Ibsen's original audiences. But we can still be struck by the force of the revelation that finally shocks Nora into awareness — the revelation that the sacrifice she made (and has been making) for Helmer, of which she is so proud, <u>he</u> views as shameful; that he's not thankful that Nora saved his life but angry that she's threatened his reputation. Then, once the danger has passed, Helmer acts as if nothing has happened. He's oblivious to the significance of his original reaction and to its impact on Nora. He waxes philosophical about the joys of forgiving one's wife — "She becomes his property in a double sense. . . ." — and he thinks the only problem is that Nora doesn't yet believe he's forgiven her. (You might ask students whether they think Helmer is capable of changing, and under what conditions.)

Some critics question — and students will likely be eager to discuss this — whether the Nora we've seen throughout the play is capable of those magnificent speeches and that bold act at the end. (The "contraband" macaroons are certainly an early sign of defiance as, of course, is Nora's secret borrowing from Krogstad.) Some have also argued that Ibsen's depiction of Nora as so thoroughly childlike through so much of the play undercuts the play's critique of sexism, but one might better argue that this strengthens it, by demonstrating what this marriage (as well as her upbringing by her father) has forced Nora to become. Nora's departure is thus absolutely necessary. That departure is also extremely courageous, for in the lives of Mrs. Linden and the nurse Anna, Nora has seen what a woman on her own can face.

The relationship between Mrs. Linden and Nils Krogstad offers an important contrast to the Torvalds' marriage. Theirs will likely be an honest marriage, a marriage of equals, and will probably make them both better people (whereas marriage has undoubtedly diminished both Helmer and Nora). The role of Dr. Rank in the play is somewhat problematical, and you might simply ask students why he's there. Among other things, he's the friend to Nora that Helmer is not; she can talk to him in ways that she can't talk to her husband; and so his presence highlights what's wrong with Helmer. (Helmer does not even want to hear about friends Nora had before she met him; he'd no doubt like to think that her life began when she assumed her role as his wife.) Also, Rank's impending death heightens the growing crisis in Nora's life, for it leaves her even more alone with Helmer. And Rank lives in the deterministic grip of fate (thanks to his father) while Nora is trying to break out.

Susan Glaspell, "Trifles"

The women in this play, concerned with "trifles," can see what the men, focused on "awful important things," cannot see. The clues are all in the kitchen, and in the relationship between John and Minnie Wright. The County Attorney keeps postponing any discussion of John Wright's nature and then finds himself, at the end, still unable to establish a "motive." Many of the ironies in the play grow out of the men's underestimating the women; from time to time the men pass through the kitchen, punctuating with condescending remarks the conversation of the two women, who are in the process of solving the puzzle that the men cannot solve. Mrs. Hale and Mrs. Peters cover up the murder for many reasons, among them that Mrs. Hale feels guilty for not having visited Minnie Wright more; that she and Mrs. Peters pity her, caged and stifled as she's been; that looking through her kitchen, they come to identify with her ("We all go through the same things," says Mrs. Hale); and that prodded by the patronizing attitude of the men, they come to feel a certain solidarity as women with the beleaguered former Minnie Foster. Their anger is suggested by Mrs. Hale's subtle taunt — "knot it" —at the end. Mrs. Peters, "married to the law," does not find all this easy, but ultimately she, like Mrs. Hale, finds it necessary. Students should have much to say about this play which, after all, sympathetically portrays an attempt (probably successful) to cover up a murder.

NONFICTION

Plato, from <u>The Symposium</u>

This parable about Love offers a somewhat different origin myth than does the Biblical "Genesis." And you might ask students to read the Biblical myth and compare the two. While "Genesis" makes man the original being and woman a second thought, made from a piece of man, Aristophanes' story posits an equality — each half is looking for its other half. He does have an argument here and it is in favor of love between males as the highest form of love. What do students think about his position that "such boys and lads are the best of their generation, because they are the most manly"? The argument in that paragraph has a somewhat circular quality. Aristophanes' remarks about women who love women seems carefully neutral. His tone when he talks in that paragraph about heterosexuals is not so neutral, however. <u>The Symposium</u> is written from a male homosexual perspective and Aristophanes is relating this parable to a group of men who also see love between men as the highest form of love; thus the assumptions of <u>The Symposium</u> will probably challenge heterosexual readers who are used to being the norm. You might want to explore with students how it feels to be in a world (this text) where the norms of most of them are not assumed to be correct and are not taken for granted — does it make them feel disoriented, bewildered, angry, resistant, thoughtful? In addition, you might want to think about what Plato is suggesting about Love as the force which moves the world. Freud thought sex did it; is Aristophanes here simply referring to sex? Do students agree with the paragraph in which Hephaestus asks, "Is the object of your desire to be always together as much as possible. . . " Is it, in fact, love that makes the world go round?

Virginia Woolf, "Shakespeare's Sister"

This piece is a short excerpt from Woolf's book length essay about women and the writing of fiction, <u>A Room of One's Own</u>. Her thesis in that book is that a woman must have financial independence and a room of her own if she is to be able to write. Through the book, she uses the comparison/contrast method to demonstrate historically women's relative poverty and lack of encouragement, women's training to nurture everyone but themselves, and male control of the literary and intellectual establishment. She does this through literary devices of metaphor, scene, and incident: a sumptuous luncheon at a men's college vs. a frugal dinner at a women's college, and a callow but confident young male researcher seated next to her, fumbling through card catalogs at the library looking for the "truth" about women and fiction, are two examples.

In this short piece Woolf creates a character, Shakespeare's sister Judith, and tells the story of the brief tormented life of an imaginary young woman of genius in the Elizabethan Age, implicitly contrasting Judith's story to Shakespeare's own. Throughout, Woolf's interest is in the material, social/historical, and psychological conditions that further or impede the development of artistic creativity. In this sketch of Judith, what are the conditions that keep her from developing her gift? Though Woolf's focus is mostly on gender, we might consider social class (Woolf mentions this briefly) and race in regard to the question of nurturing artistic creativity, or indeed human potential of any sort. Conversely, what conditions help to develop creativity? Students might wish to discuss what the ideal conditions would be. And there might be some arguments advanced in class discussion that struggle and adversity produce good writing. Or that people of talent will prevail no matter what the conditions (the cream-rises-to-the-top theory of success). What are the limits of all these different viewpoints?

Sojourner Truth, "Ain't I a Woman"

In this brief speech, Sojourner Truth, with sharp wit and gentle humor, disposes of a few of the standard justifications for the subordination of women. The first is that women are weaker: while they may not have equal rights, they do have privileges ("the best place everywhere"), and should be grateful. Sojourner Truth, of course, is neither weak nor privileged, as indicated by her strong arm and her history of labor and grief. To the claim that women are intellectually inferior, she replies that it would be "mean" to take away "women's rights or negro's rights" on such grounds, but the more important counterargument is the example of her own intelligence, hardly a mere "pint." The Bible, of course, has been used to justify many things, and Sojourner Truth's clever exegesis towards the end turns traditional sexist interpretations on their head.

Judy Brady, "I Want a Wife"

You might use "I Want A Wife" to discuss the effectiveness of humor in constructing political arguments or in persuasive writing of any kind. How does the form of this essay make it both palatable and accessible to large numbers of people? How does a writer achieve the transformation of anger (and a sense of injustice) into humor?

What kind of portrait of a husband emerges from Brady's essay? Why does she say all this occurs to her while she's ironing? Note that Tillie Olsen's first person short story, "I Stand Here Ironing," begins also with a woman (that time a mother) standing at an ironing board. Like Woolf in her piece on Shakespeare's sister Judith, Brady uses the comparison/contrast method to make her argument: point by point the enviable position a husband occupies in this society is compared to that of his wife.

Students might also consider this essay alongside Susan Griffin's prose poem, "This is the Story of a Day in the Life of a Woman Trying." Griffin too details her day, there as a single mother who is at the same time trying to be a writer, and also brings in a male friend for purposes of contrast. See the discussion of Brady's essay in "How Nonfiction Works."

MONEY AND WORK

We have sometimes arranged an entire introductory writing course around the subject of work, using some of the selections in this section along with Studs Terkel's Working, feature films like Chaplin's Modern Times, and documentary films like Union Maids and The Life and Times of Rosie the Riveter. Assignments have included: writing about a good or a bad job experience students have had, writing a first person narrative from the perspective of an unemployed or a street person, writing a research paper about the kind of work a student would like to go into, as well as writing papers about the literary texts.

Below are a number of themes around which the selections might be grouped. Others will probably occur to you. Unemployment and its stresses are dealt with in the Kromer, LeSueur, and Wright pieces; these three are also set during the Great Depression. Alienated vs. satisfying labor is the subject of a number of selections: Traven's "Assembly Line" and Berlin's "Manual for Cleaning Women," Miller's Death of a Salesman, Roethke's "Dolor," Mbuli's "The Miners," Sandburg's "Chicago," and perhaps Hardy's "The Ruined Maid," though that ironic poem looks at the rewards the job of prostitute brings rather than at the work itself. The need for recognition of one's labor, the need to have one's work valued, is a subject of Brecht's "A Worker Reads History," Miller's Death of a Salesman, Wright's "The Man Who Went to Chicago," and perhaps Tillie Olsen's "I Stand Here Ironing." Writing as work comes up in poems by Jordan and Griffin. Money and what it can buy are at the center of Hansberry's A Raisin in the Sun, Bambara's "The Lesson," Faulkner's "Spotted Horses," and Wendy Rose's "Three Thousand Dollar Death Song." Social class and cross-class tensions, as well as working-class pride, are an aspect of many of these selections: Walker's "Everyday Use," Olsen's "I Stand Here Ironing," the poems by Alvarez, Brecht, Swift, Baca, Hardy, Sáenz. In the poems by Hughes and Brooks, as in Wright's "The Man Who Went to Chicago," racism merges with classism as a force and a subject. The effect of money and work issues on self-esteem and on family and other personal relations is a part of most of the selections; see especially Olsen's "I Stand Here Ironing," Miller's Death of a Salesman, Hansberry's A Raisin in the Sun, and Walker's "Everyday Use." What has been traditionally seen as women's work (domestic labor, motherhood, and prostitution) comes up in "I Stand Here Ironing, "Everyday Use," "The Ruined Maid," "Dolor," "Bronzeville Woman in a Red Hat," "Manual for Cleaning Women," and the selection from Angelou's I Know Why the Caged Bird Sings. The additional poems provide further views of the complex interaction of work and money and include selections from British, German, Turkish, Mexican, and African writers. See also the songs included here.

The other sections can supplement what is included in Money and Work. Some of the selections in Women and Men deal with work: Updike's "A & P," Broumas's "Cinderella," McKay's "The Harlem Dancer," Wakoski's "Slicing Oranges for Jeremiah," Sojourner Truth's "Ain't I a Woman." In Peace and War, you might consider selections that deal with soldiers as workers, like Kipling's "Tommy," or the situation of workers in war time, as in Brecht's "From a German War Primer." Or you might look at Atwood's poem about a job, "The Loneliness of the Military Historian." In Varieties of Protest, pieces about work include Melville's "Bartleby, the Scrivener," Zoline's "The Heat Death of the Universe" as a powerful comment on housework, Childress's play Florence about black/white relations in the south, Sillitoe's consideration of British class relations in "The Loneliness of the Long Distance Runner," and the union song "Solidarity Forever."

FICTION

Tillie Olsen, "I Stand Here Ironing"

Olsen writes in the autobiographical section of her book <u>Silences</u> that it is no accident that the first work she considered publishable begins, "I stand here ironing, and what you asked me moves tormented back and forth with the iron." As a woman who had to work to support herself and her children, she found very little time in her own life to write. However autobiographically based the writing might be, in this story (and in other pieces like Wright's "The Man Who Went to Chicago" and LeSueur's "Women on the Breadlines"), students do need to be cautioned that the "I" narrator of a piece of writing is not identical with the author.

You will probably want to bring up the issues in this story of time, guilt, responsibility, power and powerlessness, and relation to authority. Why is the setting of this meditation an ironing board? Does the mother move from guilt to understanding in the course of the story? Is there a change in or development of consciousness? Does the implied audience change at all? Our sense is that by the last paragraph, the meditation has become less a response to the teacher who was concerned about Emily, and more a prayer.

As well as the study questions and comments on this story in the "Money and Work" preface, you might want to consider the question of creativity and Emily's particular art form. How is mime, both as comedy and as a powerfully expressive form of silence, an appropriate response to the central metaphor of the story and to the narrative itself?

William Faulkner, "Spotted Horses"

"Spotted Horses" was first published separately as a short story and later in an expanded version became part of the novel <u>The Hamlet</u>, the first of Faulkner's Snopes Trilogy. Faulkner had in earlier novels like <u>The Sound and the Fury</u> portrayed the decay of a southern aristocracy. There's no "aristocracy" <u>per se</u> in this story, but we do see an undercurrent of the old order, represented by Varner, beginning to be pushed out by the new, represented by Flem Snopes. In this story and in the rest of the Snopes Trilogy, Faulkner chronicles the rise of a new Southern middle class in the form of the "tribe" of Snopeses, with Flem at their head — though "chronicles" is not quite the word, since Faulkner's Snopeses are not entirely realistic but have that grotesque quality of characterization that often occurs in Southern novels (Carson McCullers, Flannery O'Connor).

Part of the reason that Flem can win in this story is that he has no code of ethics that the rest of the community can comprehend. The Armstids' encounter with Flem's implacability makes that clear. Flem is an entirely profit oriented, individualistic entrepreneur with no sense of responsibility to the community. Figuring out what the unwritten code of ethics and behavior is here is helpful in understanding the subtle character and plot tensions in "Spotted Horses."

Another useful approach is to discuss point of view in the story. The itinerant sewing machine salesperson, Radcliffe, narrates this story and most of the Snopes Trilogy. What kind of person is he? What is his code of ethics? What is his place in the community? Note that he stays detached from the central action of horse buying, as does the other observer/commentator on the action, Mrs. Littlejohn. What is the attitude of these two characters toward the events of the story?

And what about the 'consumer madness' that sweeps the town, people's feverish desire, against their better judgment, to own one of those wild pinto ponies? What do the horses represent to people? There's some combination here of a relatively useless commodity promising to satisfy a batch of psychological needs (status? self esteem? risk and adventure? excitement? what else?) and the auction format which brings on people's gambling fever (the idea that you're going to get something for nothing, or at least a real bargain). Students might discuss contemporary luxury commodities and the way we become convinced we "need" things.

B. Traven, "Assembly Line"

This seemingly sweet little story should drive economics majors — with their notions about comparative advantage and economies of scale — quite crazy. Partly, it's about the often bemoaned conflict between commerce and art: the haggling the Indian faces at the market links him to "every artist all over the world" and the grand scheme Winthrop plans would prevent the Indian from making the baskets with his "song in them." More broadly the story suggests the potential of the profit-making impulses of a wealthy individual for turning meaningful work into alienated labor and for reorganizing a community in destructive ways. The uneducated Indian to whom Winthrop is so patronizing sees quite clearly that to organize his and his neighbors' lives around mass production of baskets would mean farming would be neglected, corn and beans would rise in price, and people might starve. Winthrop is blind to everything but the business opportunity he thinks he's chanced upon; to him, Mexico is a pathetic place until his profit calculations convince him that it "isn't so backward after all." We see in the relationship between Winthrop and the Indian a microcosm of neocolonial relations between wealthy and Third World nations — only here the Indian has the power to refuse the deal. Traven doesn't romanticize the Indian's life or his poverty, but he makes it clear that Winthrop will make things much worse.

Tom Kromer, from <u>Waiting For Nothing</u>

A writing exercise we've tried asks students to place themselves in the position of Kromer's narrator: "Imagine that you have no job, no place to live, and only $4.35 [or whatever amount seems reasonable] in your pocket. . . . Write a brief narrative (500 -1000 words) based on this situation, using first person point of view." Students often enjoy this exercise and find it relatively easy to write. It tends to bring up for them in a personally felt way issues that are central to Kromer's piece: the importance of getting basic survival needs, like food and shelter, met each day; the struggles with self esteem — a sense of failure and humiliation and anger; a look at the economic and social system from a new perspective, i.e., the bottom; the struggle, in the face of one's situation and the way other people respond to you, to maintain some sense of human dignity.

Waiting For Nothing is set and was written in the same time period as LeSueur's "Women on the Breadlines" and Wright's "The Man Who Went to Chicago" and these three together make a good unit on the early years of the Great Depression. To relieve the grimness, we like to add Charlie Chaplin's great 1936 film, Modern Times. The section from Waiting For Nothing included here is the first chapter. Eleven more follow, each one operating as a separate unit, the episodic nature of this autobiographically based novel paralleling the day-to-day experience of being down and out. The twelve chapters touch upon experiences and issues like mission houses, male prostitution, riding the rails, hobo jungles, violence among stiffs, con games, getting busted and dealing ith the courts, and some rare moments of comradeship and affection in what is basically a solitary, survival-from-day-to-day kind of life.

Toni Cade Bambara, "The Lesson"

Sylvia hears part of the lesson early on: "how money ain't divided up right in this country." On their outing, she and her friends mainly discover how little they have compared to others, but also how excessive what others have is: the absurdly expensive toys, the fur coat ostentatiously worn in summer ("White folks crazy"). The noisy kids grow suddenly quiet when they enter F.A.O. Schwarz, just as Sylvia and Sugar did the time they "crashed" their way into a Catholic church; consumerism is America's true religion, but the church isn't open to all. Despite their poverty now, despite the even tougher problems they will soon face as adults trying to make their way in a racist society, Sylvia and her friends are not pathetic; their youthful playfulness, their wise-cracking humor, their boundless energy make them more than just victims. Tough and vulnerable at once, Sylvia tries to resist Miss Moore's lesson — what kid would want to think about all that? — but she grows angry for reasons she can't quite understand and she gets "a headache for thinkin so hard." The lesson is not just an intellectual one: Miss Moore wants these children not only to understand their situation but to grow up to "demand their share of the pie." By the end, Sugar has enunciated the lesson ("this is not much of a democracy") but Sylvia has truly felt it and been changed by it. Students, whatever their social class, should have much to say about how they learned this or a related lesson.

Lucia Berlin, "Manual for Cleaning Women"

The story was originally published as a chapbook under this title, then republished twice under the title "Maggie May," and finally appeared in Berlin's latest collection of stories, Homesick, under the original title. Does the title make a difference in how we read the story? You could ask students to collect Maggie's explicit advice to cleaning women. Some people in your class may have worked as housecleaners; you might ask whether Maggie's advice makes good sense. Some people in your class, on the other hand, may have employed (or their parents may have employed) housecleaners. How do they feel about Maggie's advice and about her characterizations of her employers?

This story works well alongside the excerpt from Angelou's I Know Why the Caged Bird Sings, Brooks's "Bronzeville Woman in a Red Hat," Sáenz's "Journeys," and to some extent Alvarez's "Homecoming," all of which consider domestic work and the social class relations between employer and employee. Unlike in Angelou and Brooks, where the domestic worker is Black, and in Sáenz, where she is Mexican, Berlin's Maggie is White/Anglo. Does that make any difference in her attitude toward her work and her employers (and in their attitude toward and treatment of her)? What kind of life is Maggie leading and how do the setting(s) in the story — the various workplaces, the bus rides, the view into Mill and Addie's laundry —contribute to our sense of Maggie's life and where she is in that life?

Alice Walker, "Everyday Use"

As in Berlin's "Manual for Cleaning Women," Freeman's "A Mistaken Charity," and the excerpt from Angelou's I Know Why the Caged Bird Sings, the tension in "Everyday Use" is located in an encounter across social class. Unlike the other two, however, Walker's story takes place within a family and in some ways that makes the tensions more subtle, complicated, and moving. What happens when one member of a family becomes upwardly mobile and leaves? Here Walker places the action on a visit home by Dee, the oldest daughter, who went off to college, became middle class, and, further, wants to redefine her identity in relation to an African rather than an African-American heritage.

What are the cluster of motivations that impel Dee to return home? What does she want from this visit: what kind of statement is she trying to make to her family; what does she want from them to take away with her to further construct her new identity? The overt struggle in the story is over family artifacts like the butter churn and especially the quilts, which Dee would hang on the wall as examples of folk art (the art of her folk), but which her sister Maggie would use every day and, further, knows how to make. The first thing Dee does, even before she properly greets her family, is to take some "quaint" snapshots of the family, the yard, the cow, and the house she hated. The point of view is the mother's. How does the mother's sense of herself, her daughters, her family history develop over the afternoon the story covers?

How people in the class feel about Dee often becomes a focus of discussion: whether they have any sympathy for her or see her as shallow and unredeemable. In the journal excerpts in the "Literature and the Writing Process" section is an example of one student's attempt to come to terms with her uneasiness about dismissing Dee. In this context, it is interesting to remember that Walker herself, as the daughter who left her working class rural family, went to college, and became a successful writer, most closely approximates Dee's position in the story.

POETRY

Bertolt Brecht, "A Worker Reads History"

Students, particularly working-class students, usually have a great deal to say about this poem. Their parents probably worked hard and got little recognition for it; maybe they themselves are in the same position. You might ask them for contemporary examples to illustrate Brecht's point. The poem is about how history is constructed; you might ask what their history textbooks were like in high school and what kind of history the worker in the poem might write. Of course, Brecht and his worker have their own limitations as historians and social critics: except perhaps for their contribution to the "tears" shed, women, and their work, are invisible in "A Worker Reads History."

Jonathan Swift, "A Description of the Morning"

In heroic couplets Swift paints a sort of mock pastoral picture of the urban morning — not a beautiful, peaceful site of rural goodness, but a grimy, sordid place where people work. As the day unfolds, so do the ironies: the maid <u>unmakes</u> a bed; the jailer has let prisoners loose. Social class differences stand out: the "master" exploits Betty; his "lordship" is still lord despite his debts while no doubt lower-class criminals have to pay the costs of their imprisonment.

Thomas Hardy, "The Ruined Maid"

You can see from Hardy's ironical and practical attitude toward prostitution in this poem why he was constantly at odds with Victorian morality and in struggles with editorial censorship. This is a vision of prostitution as class mobility, a few steps up and out of hard, dull, poverty stricken, trapped, hand roughening farm work into urban, lively, well dressed, well spoken relative independence and prosperity. The price is being "ruined," but the "I" of the poem seems quite taken with Melia's transformation. Of course, Hardy doesn't deal here with the dangers, internalized shame, and often lousy working conditions of the job. Theodore Dreiser, in Sister Carrie (1900), similarly shocked the American reading public with his account of a young country woman who came to the city, traded sex for social mobility and made a success of her life.

Wendy Rose, "Three Thousand Dollar Death Song"

As the speaker (at the start) tries to imagine what form the $3,000 might take, we grow increasingly aware of what Native Americans have been reduced to and of the callous cruelty of those responsible. As the speaker continues to contemplate the invoice, she begins to identify with the skeletons. It's not only bodies that have been destroyed, but a whole culture; beadwork, medicine bundles, bridles have also been reduced to commodities; the white conquerors have turned "our dead into specimens, our history/into dust, our survivors into clowns." The poem ends with the speaker's vision of rebirth and revenge, of the repossession of "a universe/of stolen things." Students trying to understand the intensity of Rose's feelings might read "The Butchering at Wounded Knee" by Black Elk in the "Peace and War" section.

Theodore Roethke, "Dolor"

See the discussion of the sound effects Roethke uses in this poem in "How Poetry Works." What is the effect when read aloud of the long lines and polysyllabic words in "Dolor"? What is the effect too of the listing, piling up of images of clerical work? Roethke not only gives you images and a sound pattern to structure an emotional response, but (unusual in a modern poet) tells you what that response should be, through abstract words like "sadness," "misery" "desolation," "lonely," "pathos," " dangerous," and "tedium." This poem would not tend to entice one into low level office work as a career, and we have seen this poem tacked on to the bulletin boards of at least two English department secretarial offices. What is it about this kind of work that is most alienating: its lack of control, its dearth of creativity, its meaninglessness, its repetitiousness, something else? And Roethke begins by identifying himself with the still and static inhabitants of this setting, by saying, "I have known. . ."; but to what extent is this poet's view of office work different from that of someone (usually a woman) whose main work and means of making a living it is?

Carl Sandburg, "Chicago"

Though "Hog Butcher for the World" is not so impressive today as it once was, students will still feel the power of the speaker's pride in his city, a pride based mainly on the work done there. It's a macho sort of bragging ("a tall bold slugger set vivid against the little soft cities"), a pride that may gloss too easily over what (the speaker admits) is wrong with Chicago. His romanticizing of hard physical labor (think of Upton Sinclair's The Jungle) and his ability to keep on celebrating the city despite those "marks of wanton hunger" on the faces of some of its citizens suggest the speaker himself has probably escaped hunger and drudgery.

Julia Alvarez, "Homecoming"

The speaker of the poem comes home to the Dominican Republic from Vermont to attend a family wedding. Though she says it would be "years before I could begin to comprehend/how one does not see the maids when they pass by," she does provide for us, remembering this scene, the perspective of someone both inside and outside the world of wealth the poem describes. This world includes the upper-class guests, the servants, the groom's family from Minnesota, the bride's family, and the speaker of the poem. Her uncle tries to seduce her to come back, repeating "all this is yours." The uncle is portrayed in subtly disturbing ways; he seems in several senses to embody the corrupt core of this scene. The center of the poem is the speaker's realization (at the time of writing) of the social stratification which she once took for granted to the extent that she didn't even see the men and women who worked in her family's house. Ironically, the maids and workmen end up eating the cake replica of the house, since by the time the cake is served the guests are too stuffed from their earlier culinary excesses to eat any of it. There are several image clusters which are worth exploring in themselves and in connection with each other: the wedding celebration preparations, the cake, the dancing, the sugarcane fields, the uncle, the Minnesotans, the maids and workmen. The poem to some extent fits with other pieces that consider domestic workers and social class.

Gwendolyn Brooks, "Bronzeville Woman in a Red Hat"

This poem is from Brooks's volume, <u>The Bean Eaters</u>. In many of her poems from that volume, Brooks captures vividly commonplace situations, either within the black community or in black/white relations. She has a genius for: 1) telling stories in poetic form, creating narratives and characters; 2) controlling point of view to create new insight into these situations; and 3) doing so in a measured and nonrhetorical way that moves her readers toward the response she wants without making them feel manipulated. Here she takes on the perspective of the white woman, Mrs. Miles, who is trying to come to terms with the new black maid she's hired to cook, clean, and take care of her child. Somehow the effect Brooks achieves through this technique is that you see Mrs. Miles's flaws with brilliant clarity, their basis in ignorance and fear, and also the tendrils of possibility in, say, her attitude toward the "red hat that was rash, but refreshing —/in a tasteless way, of course" and in her child's natural and unsocially conditioned response to the woman who is giving him comfort. You also see the Bronzeville woman's strength, humanity, and vibrancy.

William Blake, "The Chimney Sweeper"

You might begin by asking students what they know, or can infer from the poem, about the lives of children in Blake's day who worked as chimney sweepers. Many in fact were too young to pronounce "sweep" when, sometimes sold into servitude by their poor parents, they began working in those "coffins of black." In the poem, one of Blake's Songs of Innocence, Tom Dacre's dream of escape serves, ironically, to enable him to carry on the next day with this oppressive work. His innocence is to believe that if he behaves well, he'll "never want joy." Though the last line seems to echo a master's threat, the speaker, too, reveals his innocence. The poem indicts not only the cruel exploitation of these young children, but the moralizing that defends and sustains it. Readers cannot escape being implicated: it's "your chimneys" the narrator says he sweeps, and, perhaps, too, it's "their duty" to work to change these conditions. Blake wrote the poem in midst of efforts to outlaw the worst abuses of chimney sweepers.

William Wordsworth, "The World Is Too Much With Us"

It's worth focusing a while on the first seven lines of this sonnet: just what does it mean for "the world" to be "too much with us"? Then, what is it that Wordsworth is saying we have lost now that we are immersed in our materialistic pursuits? And why would he rather be a "Pagan"? Is Wordsworth suggesting that his own Christian religion is somehow implicated in the materialism he condemns? Once it is clear what the poem is saying, you might ask students if they agree that "Getting and spending, we lay waste our powers." After all, some might argue, isn't that what our "powers" are for?

Anonymous, song: "We raise de wheat"

In My Bondage and My Freedom (1855), the first of the three autobiographies he wrote, Frederick Douglass says of this song: [indent block] This is not a bad summary of the palpable injustice and fraud of slavery, giving — as it does — to the lazy and idle, the comforts which God designed should be given solely to the honest laborer.

Matthew Arnold, "West London"

The speaker in this sonnet watches an impoverished "tramp" send her daughter to beg from "labouring men" that pass by. She does not, he observes, have her daughter beg from the "rich," only from those almost as poor as she is, not from "aliens" but from "friends." He's impressed. Her "spirit towers" above her lowly material "state," he thinks, for she prefers her pride and her dignity to the "cold succour" of those who might look down at her or look through her. So great a "spirit" in one so lowly! If we could learn from her, the future would be "a better time than ours." What are the implications of the speaker's admiration? What are the politics of praising the poor for refusing to make demands on the rich? Don't discourage students from trying to re-imagine this situation and attitude in our own time.

William Carlos Williams, "The Young Housewife"

There are two characters in this poem: the poet/observer and the young housewife who is the object of his observation. She is young, shy, still wandering around in her nightgown at 10 a.m., and is not only a possession, at least conceptually and visually, of the poet, but also of her husband (she lives inside the "wooden walls of her husband's house"). Williams compares her to a fallen leaf, which initially sounds lovely even though "fallen" might seem dubious; but in subsequent lines his car crushes other fallen leaves as he passes by, bowing to her.

Berton Braley, "The Worker"

This may be considered as part of a cluster of poems in this section on relations between wage earners and bosses or owners. (Nazim Hikmet, "About Your Hands and Lies," Bertolt Brecht, "A Worker Reads History," the song "Let Them Wear Their Watches Fine," Marge Piercy,

"The market economy," Mafika Mbuli, "The Miners.") What about the last four lines of this poem; what is the worker's attitude toward his situation and his conclusions about it? Given the rest of the poem, did students expect an angrier, less patient, and more revolutionary conclusion? Written by a Colorado miner, the poem was originally published in a union magazine between 1903 and 1906.

Sarah Cleghorn, "The golf links lie so near the mill"

The irony here — that the men and the children have switched roles — does not call attention to itself (and, in fact, seems almost hidden behind the sweet simplicity of the meter and rhyme), but students will catch it sooner or later. Child labor is most likely to be found today in illegal sweatshops (probably not near golf courses) or in Third World countries, but Cleghorn's poem is hardly dated.

Fenton Johnson, "Tired"

This poem shifts mood several times; a drastic shift begins with "Throw the children into the river." The poem also mixes the personal with the very broadly political. Ask students to explain what the speaker means by "building up somebody else's civilization" and to discuss the connotations that develop around the word "civilization." This poem might be read alongside the antebellum song, "We raise de wheat."

Countee Cullen, "For a Lady I Know"

"She _even_ thinks . . ." Ask students to write a paragraph describing what else she thinks. Central to most ideology that justifies class and race inequalities is the claim that these inequalities are natural, inevitable, eternal. In Cullen's satire, they're pushed even into heaven.

Anonymous, song: "Let Them Wear Their Watches Fine"

This song might be compared with Breton Braley's "The Worker" in his presentation of the condition of working people and their relation to nonworking people. The work, here mill work, is described: the low pay, the long day, the attempt to feed and clothe a family on "little pay." Though the song is anonymous, there are indications the writer is a woman. Contrast its angry conclusion with the more emotionally ambivalent ending of "The Worker." The song has three parts; the first three stanzas from an "I" perspective introduce the speaker; stanzas 4 - 9 from a communal or "we" point of view describe the workers' lives; and stanzas 10 - 12 focus on "them," the bosses and "folks in town."

Easy Papa Johnson (Roosevelt Sykes), song "Cotton Seed Blues"

Like Braley's "The Worker," Mafika Mbuli's "The Miners," and the song "Let Them Wear Their Watches Fine," "Cotton Seed Blues" describes work conditions and the relation of the worker to the bosses, to those who own the means of production. Here the work is agricultural, probably sharecropping. The sharecropper gets the seed and other materials (often including food on credit during the growing season) from the commissary owned by the person who also owns the land. At the end of the season, the sharecropper has to take whatever the going price is for cotton and all too often ends up still in debt after the crop is made. As the song concludes, "you know no way I could win." The standard blues lyric form is used here —the first two lines of the stanza are the same and the third is a comment on or conclusion to the situation or emotion expressed in the opening two lines.

D.H. Lawrence, "City-Life"

This poem — with its horrifying image of people being pulled to and from the factory by iron hooks in their faces — offers perhaps the bleakest view in this section of the world of work. You might ask students to characterize the speaker, the "I," and also ask them what that "malignant fisherman" might represent.

Bertolt Brecht, "Song of the Invigorating Effect of Money"

Students might be misled, by the first stanza especially, into thinking this poem simply a celebration of money. To help them see Brecht's point about the connections between material conditions and one's view of the world and about the hypocrisy of the rich preaching virtue to the poor, you might focus on the last eight lines and especially on the meaning of "He whom crime's already given breaks." The "Song" is from Roundheads and Peakheads, a satirical comedy about Hitler and racism.

C. Day Lewis, "Come, live with me and be my love"

This 1935 parody needs to be read with Christopher Marlowe's poem, "The Passionate Shepherd to His Love" (in the "Women and Men" chapter). What comment is it making on Marlowe's poem? What is Day Lewis using Marlowe's poem to say about the world of the 1930s? What is the effect of the description of Depression-era troubles in the style of Marlowe's pastoral?

Robert Frost, "Two Tramps in Mud Time"

The poem is set in an ambivalent season (April in the northeast) and the speaker of the poem is in an ambivalent situation: doing work he loves — chopping wood — and knowing throughout the poem that he is going to give up that loved labor and pay the two tramps to do it instead because, after all, work is something one is supposed to do for wages. "I had no right to play/With what was another man's work for gain."

Contrast the description of nonalienated labor here and in Barbara Smith's "The Bowl" and B. Traven's "Assembly Line" with the descriptions of alienated labor in Braley's "The Worker" and the songs "Let Them Wear Their Watches Fine" and "Cotton Seed Blues." What are the factors that make work alienated vs. satisfying? Ask students to think about Frost's philosophy of work in the last stanza.

William Carlos Williams, "The Poor"

What is the speaker's attitude toward poverty? Is he sentimentalizing it? What are the details about poverty that delight him; what does he mean by "the anarchy of poverty"? How does his position as an observer allow him to take this stance? An exercise might be to rewrite the description from the point of view of someone who lives on the street — say, the old man sweeping the sidewalk.

Muriel Rukeyser, "Boy with His Hair Cut Short"

This poem from the Depression captures the defeat, the forced hopefulness, the exhaustion of the unemployed — highlighted by the youth of the boy and his sister. Ask students how each detail contributes to the mood Rukeyser is creating (and the point she is trying to make). Why the cap? Why that neon sign? Why a haircut?

Woody Guthrie, song: "Plane Wreck at Los Gatos (Deportees)"

In January 1948, an airplane carrying deported migrant farmworkers crashed on the way to Mexico. Guthrie read the news story and wrote this song. Though absolutely essential to agricultural production, the farmworkers he writes of are economically exploited and marginal to most Americans' consciousness; the speaker, a farmworker, insists on repeating their names, but on the radio they are insignificant and anonymous, "just deportees." Their apartness and powerlessness are dramatized by Guthrie's choice of pronouns. Most of the song seems to be addressed to the American people ("You" in line 3 and "your" throughout the fourth verse), a group distinct from the farmworkers ("we"), whether legal or "illegal." (You might ask students who "they" refers to.) Up until the last stanza, the speaker appears fatalistic: we died across the river in Mexico, we died working here, and now we die flying back. But the rhetorical questions in the last verse suggest that things might be otherwise, that these farmworkers might escape their second-class status and be truly integrated into American society, if only a better way can be found to grow "our" food. This song could be read alongside Jimmy Santiago Baca's "So Mexicans Are Taking Jobs From Americans."

Nazim Hikmet, "About Your Hands and Lies"

Hikmet was a Turkish poet and revolutionary who wrote a good many of his poems in Turkish jails. Another translation of the poem's title is "About Your Hands and Their Lies," which perhaps makes clearer where the lies are coming from. Ask students to notice the series of vivid similes for workers' hands, and the syntactic repetition in the "hands" section and in the "if" section later on. (André Breton in "Freedom of Love" uses a similar technique.) What details and qualities does Hikmet ascribe to the metonymical hands? Where are the lies coming from and what do they consist of? You can read this along with Braley's "The Worker" and the song "Let Them Wear Their Watches Fine."

Langston Hughes, "Ballad of the Landlord"

Part of Hughes's 1951 volume of poems about Harlem, <u>Montage of a Dream Deferred</u>, this "Ballad" explores tenant/landlord relations in poverty. The tenant complains, the landlord ignores him. The landlord says give the money you owe; the tenant says no, not until you repair the place. The conflict escalates to eviction threats and the tenant threatens to punch the landlord. At this point, the landlord calls on the power of the state and the tenant is arrested: "Judge gives Negro 90 days in county jail." Race and class oppression intersect in this poem as the black tenant learns just how little freedom he has to protest injustice. The first twenty lines of the poem are in the tenant's voice, talking to the landlord. The next four lines (in italics) are the landlord, calling on the police. Then a series of short lines, almost stage directions, as the tenant is taken to jail. The poem ends with three newspaper headlines. Hughes's poems are so easy to read one forgets how well crafted they are; have students discuss what Hughes achieves in this poem and how he does it.

Mari Evans, "When in Rome"

In this "dialogue" between a white woman and the black woman who works for her, the fact that the black woman's thoughts remain unspoken dramatizes the power relations between the two. Why does Evans begin with "Mattie dear"? Is there any significance to "Rome" beyond the allusion to the saying, "When in Rome, do as the Romans do"? This poem might be read with Countee Cullen's "For a Lady I Know" and Gwendolyn Brooks's "Bronzeville Woman in a Red Hat."

Derek Walcott, "The Virgins"

This poem tells of the destructive effects of the subordination (or, perhaps, given its ironic title, prostitution) of the Virgin Islands to the tourist industry. The speaker implicitly compares what he sees to what he remembers of the past, of "life not lost to the American dream," commenting ironically, even bitterly, on what's been done to Frederiksted.

Perhaps some students have been on vacation to such a place (or are themselves from such a place); they're likely to have stories of the striking contrasts between the accommodations for tourists and the living conditions of most of its citizens.

Mafika Mbuli, "The Miners"

This South African poem about working in a gold mine can be read along with other poems about alienated work. What is a life spent in the kind of work Mbuli describes like; what are the details he gives us? Aside from the danger and the exhaustion, the worst effect Mbuli points at is the mental numbness, the dazed eyes, the sleepwalking through the day. Students might wish to recall work experiences (even perhaps sitting in classrooms) where this alienation and numbness has set in.

Marge Piercy, "To Be of Use"

Like Barbara Smith's "The Bowl" and Robert Frost's "Two Tramps in Mud Time," this poem images nonalienated work. The first three stanzas describe the people who do such work and the eager, patient, passionate process of engaged work. The fourth stanza mentions what we might now think of as aesthetic objects — Greek amphoras, Hopi vases — but which were made to be used. In this context, students might think of this poem in relation to Alice Walker's story, "Everyday Use." Class discussion might consider Piercy's last two lines and what she means by "real" work.

Barbara Smith, "The Bowl"

Like Piercy's "To Be of Use" and Frost's "Two Tramps in Mud Time," "The Bowl" is about satisfying work, here making bread for one's friends. No mention of money here. Would the bread baking be as satisfying if the speaker did it for a living? Piercy doesn't mention money in her poem either and Frost's poem is centered on the distinction between work for love and work for money ("need"). What does Smith mean in the line "suddenly work is ritual"? Students could compare the bowl in this poem, and the way it represents a female history and tradition, with the mortar and pestle in Audre Lorde's <u>Zami</u>.

Susan Griffin, "This is the Story of the Day in the Life of a Woman Trying"

This is a narrative and prose poem like William Carpenter's "Rain" and Carolyn Forché's "The Colonel". Griffin uses a lot of compound sentences in this poem and begins a number of sentences with "and." What effect does that have? What are the conditions of life for a single mother trying to support herself and a child as well as trying to pursue her own vocation of writing? As in Tillie Olsen's story, "I Stand Here Ironing," time and money are matters of importance since there is so little of either. Olsen says in her book <u>Silences</u> something about motherhood meaning that one is "constantly interruptible." Ask students to list the times the speaker of the poem is interrupted in her writing. What about her self doubts about her writing? About whether she has anything to say? About whether what she has to say, her subject matter, is what anyone would want to hear? What is the function of the incident where her male writer friend comes to visit? Also compare this poem to Jordan's "Free Flight," another poem about a woman trying to write.

Laureen Mar, "My Mother, Who Came From China, Where She Never Saw Snow"

The picturesque 'American dream' myth includes not just wealth and success earned through hard work, but wonders of all kinds only dreamed of in the old country. But the speaker's mother, despite her years of hard work, still labors at an oppressive job for minimal wages — making ski coats so others can play in the snow that she now can see. Why is it "frightening how fast she works"? Students from immigrant families may have a great deal to say about this poem.

Marge Piercy, "The market economy"

Don't let students forget to incorporate the title of this poem into their interpretations. Piercy's point is not that every good thing has its bad aspects, or that there's no such thing as a free lunch, but rather that in a society based on a market economy, on the operations of the market (businesses trying to maximize profit, etc.), social choices are made that no sane individual would make. The "free market" offers us, especially if we are not wealthy, much less freedom of choice than we are asked to believe we have.

Judy Grahn, "Ella, in a square apron, along Highway 80"

This is the second of seven portraits of women in Grahn's 1969 sequence, The Common Woman Poems. The other portraits include Helen, an aggressive and hard edged woman executive; Nadine, an inner city woman who holds her neighborhood together; Carol, a closeted lesbian; Detroit Annie, a wanderer who may be slightly crazy; Margaret, now a housewife, who was fired for trying to organize a union at her workplace; and Vera, an old woman who's had a hard life but still has hope. Each poem in the sequence ends with a comparison, like the rattlesnake in this poem, that defines the common woman in images that are powerful, strong, angry, and often dangerous. How is Ella angry and dangerous? How did she get that way?

Jimmy Santiago Baca, "So Mexicans Are Taking Jobs From Americans"

The poem suggests that the belief that Mexicans are taking jobs away from Americans is part of a whole complex of stereotypes, which Baca mocks in his satirically literal-minded depiction of Mexicans robbing Americans of their jobs. The politician promotes the myth that Mexicans are responsible for American unemployment (rather than, say, manufacturers who move their plants to other countries where wages are lower); "a tongue paddles through flashing waves/of lightbulbs" and says,

"They're taking our jobs away," the inclusive "our" erasing any class differences, for example between those who own and those who work in plants that move away. The speaker sees these differences quite clearly, sees racism, sees poverty, and sees a powerful few who "got all the money in this world" and find Mexicans a convenient scapegoat to offer to the public. The speaker is especially concerned with the plight of poor children, and an honest America, he believes, would say, "We are killing them."

June Jordan, "Free Flight"

"Free Flight" is available on an audio tape by Jordan; students enjoy hearing her read it. About loving oneself and honoring one's need to do creative work, about finding a space in one's life to do that creative work, Jordan's poem is exuberant and funny. As an exploration of the struggles women go through to find time to do their own work, "Free Flight" works well with Susan Griffin's prose poem, "This Is the Story of the Day in the Life of a Woman Trying" and Woolf's "Shakespeare's Sister," though Jordan's poem is more powerfully positive than either of those pieces. What does the speaker of this poem struggle with in order to love herself and write her poems? What function does food have in this poem? How about the interpolated story of the student who gives her Wagner?

Kate Rushin, "The Black Back-Ups"

Though the title, dedication, and choruses are directed to the women who sang/sing back up on popular records, the poem's center is the situation of black women who have had to do domestic work in white people's homes, who have had to leave their own children and homes to do it. The poem is written from the perspective of a woman remembering her childhood, when she wished her mother was home taking care of her, when she hated the hand-me-down clothes her mother brought home. Ask students to discuss the section of the poem on Aunt Jemima and what Rushin is doing with her running together of words. "The Black Back-ups" may be usefully studied along with Gwendolyn Brooks's "Bronzeville Woman in a Red Hat" and Countee Cullen's "For a Lady I Know." How is domestic work like and unlike the factory and mine work discussed in other poems in this section? How is it like and unlike being a "housewife," a worker (though unpaid) in one's own home? How do questions of race and class get tangled up with the kind of work that is available to you?

James Berry, "Fantasy of an African Boy"

Jamaican poet James Berry identifies here with the poor of the Third World, "we people/without money," assuming the persona of a seemingly naive African boy. The boy, far removed from the complex world of high finance, would appear unlikely to understand that world. But since he suffers the consequences of what goes on there, he understands one central fact quite well — that the "walled-round gentlemen" have the money, and he and his people do not.

Like Toni Cade Bambara's "The Lesson," Lorraine Hansberry's A Raisin in the Sun, Faulkner's "Spotted Horses," and Bertolt Brecht's "Song of the Invigorating Effect of Money," this poem is not about work or even about the relation of work and money, but simply about money. Considered the way the speaker of this poem does, money seems quite magical, a powerful talisman that can't do anything on its own; but without it nothing can be done. This brings up the issue of symbol vs. reality and how money, an abstraction, came to have so much power. What does the speaker list that one cannot do without money? You might ask students to imagine a world without money.

Maggie Anderson, "Among Elms and Maples, Morgantown, West Virginia, August, 1935"

Anderson considers a series of Walker Evans photographs here and in four companion poems in her 1986 volume Cold Comfort: "Independence Day, Terra Alta, West Virginia, 1935"; "Mining Camp Residents, West Virginia, 1935"; "Street Scene, Morgantown, West Virginia, 1935"; and "House and Graveyard, Rowlesburg, West Virginia 1935." She explores the relation between the photographer and his subjects, the formal aesthetics (often divorced from humane considerations) of the photographer, the power of the photographer (the one who sees) to define the reality of the lives of his subjects, and the poet's own relation to theses scenes, which is quite personal and very different from Evans's. By giving her own version — here, by reclaiming this as her mother's childhood house and by populating the house with her mother peeling tomatoes — Anderson takes the scene back for herself, for her invisible mother, and for other working-class people Evans photographed. But it is even more complicated, Anderson says. Though in this photo, Evans only wanted the house, in another picture he might want the speaker's mother and sister peeling tomatoes. And that would be his own definition of their lives.

Benjamin Alire Sáenz, "Journeys"

You might ask students to list all the data the poem gives us about this woman. "Journeys" gives us the sense of a person's life, while focusing on one daily event in her life, crossing the Mexican-American border on her way to and from her job as a domestic worker. How does she feel about her life? Does the last image undercut her earlier remark, "I'm happy," or the acceptance of her life that we sense. How does the border operate as a symbol in this poem?

DRAMA

Arthur Miller, Death of a Salesman

No doubt some students will have already read this play; perhaps
they can help the others follow Miller's shifts between present and past,
between reality and reverie. Students should have a great deal to say
about the pressures of parents' aspirations, the meaning and importance
of success, the best road to it, and the many other issues the play raises.
Some will probably see Willy simply as a flawed individual, the cause of
his own and his sons' problems; they may see how Biff's troubled
relationship with his father has unsuited him for the world of business,
but not how the world of business has helped create the Loman family's
problems. You might simply ask how Willy has come to be the way he is.

Willy has swallowed whole all the promises of American
business ideology. He equates happiness with success at making money,
with standing out above the crowd (as Biff does at Ebbets Field), with
"add[ing] up to something," and he equates failure with "ringing up a
zero." He believes that any man (this is a play about men), if he plays his
cards right, will end up like Dave Singleman or, if he knows the "secret,"
like Ben, who he believes "started with the clothes on his back and ended
up with diamond mines." It's significant, of course, that Willy is in sales.
"He don't put a bolt to a nut, he don't tell you the law or give you
medicine," as Charley puts it. He just tries to get someone to purchase
some (to us) unidentified product from him rather than from someone
else, and, in so doing, is always selling himself and stretching the truth.
There are other images of work in the play — Willy's father selling flutes
he crafted himself, the outdoor work that Biff enjoys so much, that "front
stoop" Willy loved working on. But Willy is a fanatical believer in a
particularly alienated kind of work, sales. And when his (never
particularly strong) selling ability falters, he's dumped, and he begins
moving towards the conclusion that he's worth more dead than alive.

You might spend some time just asking students to describe each
character, and each key relationship, in the play. Willy's false values, loud
contradictions, and stubborn assertiveness have damaged his sons and
they, in turn, are incapable of helping him when he needs help most. A
look at the women characters in the play — Linda, the long-suffering
saint, on one hand, and Miss Forsythe, Letta, and the woman in Willy's

hotel room, on the other — suggests two very traditional and limited roles for women in the very male world of this play. Willy has a growing sense of failure not only as a "salesman" but as a father to his sons, as a husband to his wife, as 'a man.'

Death of a Salesman is discussed at some length at the beginning of the section "How Drama Works" in the text.

Lorraine Hansberry, A Raisin in the Sun

College students, especially women students and especially students of typical college age, are likely to relate most easily to Beneatha Younger. She may be a bit of a snob (hence her name) and her rebelliousness may run in directions alien to some students, but her intelligence, her idealism, and her desire for independence are very appealing. Students will easily identify the sexist pressures on her — from Walter Lee, who says she should become a nurse, not a doctor ("or else just get married and be quiet"); from George Murchison, who wants her to talk less and kiss more; even from Joseph Asagai, who wants to make her his wife — but they may need to be reminded that abortion was not simply a sin in Mama's eyes, but illegal and often dangerous in the 1950s, and that giving in to either suitor could easily undermine Beneatha's plans for medical school.

Students will also have little trouble liking and admiring Ruth (for her patience, for the depth of her feelings, for her qualities as a mother) as well as Mama (for her strength, her pride, her enduring). And even the hardest-hearted student will no doubt be moved by the Youngers' struggle to get ahead, to move out of "this beat-up hole" (as Walter Lee calls their place), to overcome prejudice and move into Clybourne Park.

But the tough question — especially for white students — will no doubt be how to relate to Walter Lee. It's perhaps worth quoting at length from Ossie Davis's discussion of the play (Freedomways, Summer 1965):

> One of the biggest selling points about A Raisin in the Sun . . . was how much the Younger family was just like any other family. . . . It was good that people of all color, strata, faiths and persuasions could identify so completely with Lena Younger, and her family, and their desire to better themselves in the American way. But that's not what the play was about! The play was about Walter Lee, Lena's son, and what happened to him as a result of having his dream, his life's ambition, endlessly frustrated by poverty, and its attendant social and personal degradation. Walter Lee's dreams of "being somebody," of "making it," like everybody else, were not respectable to Mama, and not very important to us. He wanted a liquor store which would enable him to exploit the misery of his fellow slum dwellers like they were exploited by everybody else. Walter Lee is corrupted

by the materialistic aspirations at the heart of Western civilization, and his corruption is bodied forth in his petty, little dream. But it was his dream, <u>and it was all he had!</u> And that made it a matter of life or death to him . . .

It's easy to dislike Walter. He's arrogant, selfish, hot-tempered, foolish, ungrateful, even nasty to those who love him. Students will probably say that he blames everyone but himself for his problems, that he ought to work harder, save money, maybe go to night school. They may fail to distinguish between his wrongful attacks on others — his wife, his mother, his sister — and his justified anger at a racist society. It might help to ask the class to speculate on <u>how</u> Walter Lee became what he is. Why is an obviously intelligent, ambitious, energetic man in his mid-thirties still working as a chauffeur, a job he despises and feels degraded by? What's made him so bitter? What has distorted his dreams — which seem, after all, at least partly rooted in a typical desire to give his son a better life than he himself has had. Ask students to spell out just what Mama means when she says "the world done whipped him so." Walter Lee's assertion that money "is life" reflects the corruption of his aspirations that Ossie Davis talks of (compare his dreams to those of Beneatha, or of Joseph Asagai), but also the fact that the lack of money can degrade and destroy life.

NONFICTION

Meridel LeSueur, "Women on the Breadlines"

This piece of reportage is usefully taught along with Richard Wright's "The Man Who Went to Chicago" and the chapter from Tom Kromer's Waiting For Nothing. Along with this group of writing from the Great Depression, we sometimes show the 45-minute documentary film, Union Maids (1976), about women union organizers in the 1930s. "Women on the Breadlines" was originally published in the New Masses and that journal's editors appended an editorial note to LeSueur's essay calling it "defeatist" and "lacking in revolutionary spirit." You might ask students whether they do in fact find this piece "defeatist." What was LeSueur's purpose, do you think, in writing it? How might her exposé of the condition of unemployed women during the early years of the great Depression have been weakened (in emotional impact, in authenticity) if she had followed the editors' wishes? In fact, LeSueur makes a powerful and subtle argument about workers' relation to a capitalist economic structure in the paragraph about selling one's overcoat on the street, and she makes that argument in feminist terms.

"Women on the Breadlines" is also a good model of how to write a powerful argumentative essay that uses elements of narration, metaphor and characterization; see the discussion of "Women on the Breadlines" in "How Nonfiction Works."

How is the situation of unemployed women and their response to that situation different from the male narrator's in Waiting For Nothing? What are the options of men and of women in this kind of situation (in the 1930s; now)? What kind of different expectations, internal and external, operate for men and women in these two accounts? Why is that so, and have things changed?

Richard Wright, "The Man Who Went to Chicago"

This can be taught alongside LeSueur's "Women on the Breadlines" and the chapter from Kromer's Waiting For Nothing. Together, these three give a picture of the situation of black men, white women, and a white man, all from poor or working-class backgrounds, during the early years of the Great Depression. Unlike LeSueur's unemployed or marginally employed women and Kromer's "stiff" or hobo, Wright's narrator always seems to be able to find work. His situation is one of "floating labor," characterized by Harry Braverman in Labor and Monopoly Capital: The Degradation of Work in the Twentieth Century as lateral movement (within an area or from region to region) from job to job, all of them low paying and none of them with any future. Like LeSueur's "Women on the Breadlines," "The Man Who Went to Chicago" is making an argument about the worker's relation to capitalism, here specifically about the black person's situation at the bottom of the job structure. Wright uses structural elements of fiction, here episodic narration (the stories of four different jobs) to construct his argument about the external and the internalized effects of racism.

"The Man Who Went to Chicago" was first published as fiction and later was included in the second volume of Wright's autobiography, American Hunger, with two significant sections interpolated: one on his involvement with the Communist Party, the other on his work at his craft of writing.

One useful approach is to discuss how much ironic distance there is between Richard Wright as author and the first person narrator of "The Man Who Went to Chicago." While very moved by the closing hospital episode (the stair washing, the silently howling dogs, etc), students sometimes get irritated with the narrator's exploitation of black women in the insurance selling episode, his inability to trust the Jewish couple he initially works for, and his contempt for the white waitresses in the restaurant section whom he lets become representative of consumer-oriented America's "lust for trash." Assuming that Wright the author is separate from Wright the first person narrator and further that Wright the author is in control of his characterization, what might he be wanting us to learn about/from his frustrated, trapped, intelligent and angry narrator?

Maya Angelou, from <u>I Know Why the Caged Bird Sings</u>

Angelou's grandmother may have owned a store, but the young narrator of this autobiographical excerpt is hardly a "debutante." White power ensures that the black community remains a source of cheap labor for people like Mrs. Cullinan, who, even though hardly wealthy, can afford to have both Miss Glory and the narrator working in her kitchen. Despite this, the narrator relates to her employer on a human level; she may laugh at her looks, but she also pities her, and works extra hard in an effort "to make up for her barrenness." Until, that is, Mrs. Cullinan reveals that she views the narrator as a <u>thing</u> ("a sweet little thing," admittedly), choosing to change her name to Mary for her own convenience. Young Angelou may think "whitefolks" are "strange" and may view Mr. Cullinan as just another faceless white man, but her views of the other race are not backed by power, the way Mrs. Cullinan's are. This power is so pervasive that those under its influence often identify with the very people who oppress them. The narrator, only ten, has already internalized white standards of beauty (as embodied in the two Coleman girls) and Miss Glory, having toiled twenty years for the Cullinans, speaks, at the end, of "our Virginia dishes." Mrs. Cullinan, however, never loses sight of the distinctions between herself and her servants. "Clumsy little black nigger," she shouts at the narrator, and then throws a piece of broken crockery, which, interestingly, hits Miss Glory instead.

PEACE AND WAR

The majority of the selections here are from the twentieth century, but a few precede the First World War, such as Bierce's Civil War story, Black Elk's "The Butchering at Wounded Knee," and several of the additional poems — Sappho's "To an Army wife, in Sardis" and the poems by Lovelace, Milton, Whitman, and Tennyson. Several of the pieces concern the First World War, including Toni Morrison's "1919" (from Sula), Wilfred Owen's poem, "Dulce et Decorum Est," and some of the additional poems. Ray Bradbury's "August 2026: There Will Come Soft Rains" and Yōko Õta's "Fireflies" are written in the aftermath of the Second World War and in the face of the reality of nuclear war, which Carmen Tafolla's poem "How Shall I Tell You?" also considers. Kaminsky's play, In the Traffic of a Targeted City, although written in the 1980s, is in part based on the diaries of Hiroshima survivors. Margaret Drabble's story "The Gifts of War," set in London at the time of the Vietnam War, is heavy with memory of World War II.

The Vietnam War provoked the writing of Barthelme's "Report," Levertov's "Life at War," Kovic's Born on the Fourth of July, King's "A Time to Break Silence," Erdrich's "The Red Convertible," Lady Borton's essay "Wars Past and Wars Present," and poems such as Bruce Weigl's "Song of Napalm" and Nguyen Lam Son's "Can Tho." Carolyn Forché's "The Colonel" is set is El Salvador, Otto Orban's "Chile" in that country, and Joy Harjo's "Resurrection" in Nicaragua.

Attitudes toward war vary in these selections, though we have included more anti-war than pro-war pieces. Whitman's "The Dying Veteran" and Tennyson's "The Charge of the Light Brigade" praise war as an occasion for heroism, patriotism, and/or male bonding. Cummings satirizes patriotism in "'next to of course god america i." Bob Dylan in "With God on Our Side" and Margaret Atwood in "at first i was given centuries" and "The Loneliness of the Military Historian" take a historical overview of war. Rukeyser in "Waking This Morning" considers the problem of how to be nonviolent in a violent world.

Another way to group the selections is by theme: 1) the effects of war on the combatants, as in the Morrison, Kovic, Black Elk, Bierce, Erdrich, King, Borton, Weigl, and Owen pieces; 2) the effects of war on civilians and other bystanders, as in the Atwood, Õta, Levertov, and Kaminsky selections; 3) attitudes toward war, for and against, as in the selections by Dylan, Levertov, Atwood, cummings, Forché, Owen, Barthelme, Kaminsky, Tennyson, and King (perhaps Drabble's "The Gifts of War," about war toys for children, fits here too); 4) women's perspectives on war, specifically in Atwood, Lowell, Dunbar-Nelson, Tsvetayeva, Sappho, Brooks, Harjo, and Grahn — though it also might be interesting to look at poems by men and by women not obviously written with a conscious gender focus.

As an additional resource, you might use some of the anti-war or anti-violence pieces in Varieties of Protest: McKay's "If We Must Die," cummings's "i sing of Olaf glad and big," Neruda's "Ode to Federico García Lorca," parts of Grahn's "A Woman is Talking to Death," and Thoreau's "Civil Disobedience."

Students might know very little, and that little only the official version, about any of the wars written about here. A number of films have been released about the Vietnam War in the past decade or so. We find it useful to supplement the literature with an occasional film, either one that is close to the facts or one that, like many of the World War I or World War II films, so mythologizes those wars that putting such a film next to a selection like "Dulce et Decorum Est" or "1919" provides a sharp contrast. Kovic's Born on the Fourth of July is, of course, also a film.

In teaching these selections and themes, you can expect a range of opinions and emotions to surface. This section is only slightly less volatile than the one on Women and Men. The students' (particularly the male students') feelings about honor, patriotism, bravery, and so on will probably emerge and one needs to be careful, gentle, and open about letting people express their opinions without letting them trample all over each other or feel that their own beliefs are being stepped on. As with the Women and Men section, a lot of energy gets released by this subject and, with care, it can be channeled into exciting class discussions and good writing.

FICTION

Ray Bradbury, "August 2026: There Will Come Soft Rains"

This is part of Bradbury's sequence of stories collected in The Martian Chronicles (1950), about the U.S. "invasion" and colonization of Mars. The telepathic and peace-loving Martians are finally decimated by measles, which they catch from the Americans, and in a number of ways Bradbury recapitulates, in 20th century capitalistic terms, the wresting of America from its native inhabitants. Meanwhile, back on Earth, a nuclear war is heating up. (The Martian Chronicles was written in the years immediately after the atomic bombs were dropped on Hiroshima and Nagasaki). "There Will Come Soft Rains" is set in the aftermath of a nuclear war that destroys most life on this planet. The story is unusual in having no human characters (the traces of the family who lived there are imprinted on the walls). What we witness is the running down (dying) of a fully mechanical house and somehow it's appropriate that what last longest are not human beings but their technology. Readers do respond to this "death" with emotions more appropriate to the death of a person, so to what extent and how successfully does Bradbury personify the house? Our sense is that he doesn't personify it in the strict sense of the word. Yet how does he give the house life and personality? You could compare the use of time as structuring device here and in Pamela Zoline's "The Heat Death of the Universe" ("Varieties of Protest"), which is also a science fiction story.

Ambrose Bierce, "An Occurrence at Owl Creek Bridge"

The story opens with a cool, distant, quite detailed description of the mechanism that the military "executioners" of an unnamed man will be using to hang him. But soon we're identifying with this next victim of war. He's a "slave owner," "ardently devoted to the Southern cause," but his eyes have "a kindly expression," he loves his wife and children, and he's brave. The full, often lush descriptions of his sensory experiences — what he sees, hears, feels — remind us of what is destroyed when a human being is killed, and his fierce, almost frantic desire to escape and live are in sharp contrast with the formality and mechanical precision of the execution at the start. Even if we have already read this much anthologized story (or catch the many clues in Part III), we are brought up sharply at the end. The critic mentioned in the first "Writing Exercise" is F.J. Logan, whose article "The Wry Seriousness of 'Owl Creek Bridge'" appears in Critical Essays on Ambrose Bierce, edited by Cathy N. Davidson.

Toni Morrison, "1919"

"1919" is a chapter of Morrison's second novel, Sula (1973). Like Owen's "Dulce et Decorum Est," the first section of "1919" is a good description of actual warfare during World War I. But most of this story is about the after effects of battle on the combatants. Shadrack has what has come to be called post traumatic stress syndrome. He has been in the hospital a year before finally being released not because he is cured but because they need the space for other patients. He can't seem to control his hands which have a tendency to grow monstrously and to attach themselves to things like his shoelaces. (The section where Shadrack is sitting on the curb trying to take off his shoes and finally breaks down is a succinct portrayal of what it is like to lose one's sense of who one is.) Shadrack also needs very much for phenomena to remain separated inside definite boundary lines, like the food on his sectioned hospital plate. This need for an order which separates and contains is what leads Shadrack to the idea of instituting National Suicide Day.

"It had to do with making a place for fear as a way of controlling it.. . . It was not death or dying that frightened him, but the unexpectedness of both. In sorting it all out, he hit on the notion that if one day a year were devoted to it, everybody could get it out of the way and the rest of the year would be safe and free."

What do students think of the way the town accepts Shadrack and National Suicide Day? Compare this example of living with the psychological effects of war with selections by Weigl, Kovic, Borton, Erdrich. Why does Shadrack survive while, for example, the protagonist of Erdrich's "The Red Convertible" does not?

Yōko Ōta, "Fireflies"

It might be interesting to compare Ray Bradbury's whimsical though sad account of the aftermath of a nuclear war, "August 2026: There Will Come Soft Rains," with Ōta's account of the real thing. Written by a survivor eight years after the atomic bomb was dropped on Hiroshima, Ōta's account is much less neatly structured than Bradbury's fantasy. The narrator is a writer who revisits Hiroshima to observe and gather material; impressions come at her from a variety of directions and in a variety of forms — a radiation-burned stone wall, interviews with medical personnel treating the survivors, her sister's shack and the slugs that invade it, the fireflies as well as the slugs that she concludes are the ghosts of soldiers, and especially the radiation-deformed young woman, Mitsuko, who seems to have a centered sense of self and to have accepted who she is, but who unsettles everyone else. Mitsuko, along with the slugs and the wall and finally the fireflies, becomes symbolic of the horror of nuclear war and in some sense also the triumph of the human spirit. The narrator says at the end, "That is a frank expression of the way I felt." Does that refer just to the last bit — about the fireflies and the slugs — or to the whole account? Does the narrator change from beginning to end in "Fireflies"? If so, what changes her? In addition to the Bradbury story, "Fireflies" might be grouped with Marc Kaminsky's play, In the Traffic of a Targeted City, part of which is set in Hiroshima at the time of the bomb and based on accounts by survivors.

Louise Erdrich, "The Red Convertible"

Erdrich's story could be grouped with other pieces in this section about the aftereffects of war on returning soldiers, some of which deal with physical trauma as well as the psychological trauma —post traumatic stress syndrome — of war: Kovic's Born on the Fourth of July, Sassoon's "Does It Matter?", Weigl's "Song of Napalm," and Borton's "Wars Past and Wars Present." Henry Jr. in this story isn't physically wounded; how is he psychologically wounded? How is what he goes through like and unlike the experiences of veterans with physical trauma? Another approach might be to do a cluster on the Vietnam War and its consequences for individuals, putting "The Red Convertible" with Barthelme's "Report," Kovic's Born on the Fourth of July, Levertov's "Life At War," Grahn's "Vietnamese Woman Speaking to an American Soldier," the anonymous "Americans Are Not Beautiful" and Martin

Luther King Jr.'s "A Time to Break Silence." In terms of form, you might focus on the ways Erdrich identifies Henry Jr. with the red convertible and the ways she gives the car a life and a personality. The car becomes an indirect way the narrator relates to his brother; the relationship between the two of them becomes in some ways displaced onto the car, which mediates between them, especially when Henry comes home from Vietnam and his family can't reach him. The work on the car his brother arranges in the hope it will heal Henry becomes the one task Henry completes before he commits suicide. You could ask students to focus on the final scene where the car and Henry both drown. Or you could ask students to select one of the separate incidents in the story — buying the car, going to Alaska with Susy, Henry's biting through his lip, the picture of Henry — and discuss or write about how each of these helps to develop the story. Or, more ambitiously, students might try writing another short incident that they feel would also develop Erdrich's story.

Donald Barthelme, "Report"

Students may need to read this one twice. But once they begin to grasp what Barthelme is up to, they should find this satire funny and incisive. The chief engineer exemplifies the kind of technocratic mentality that could kill us all, the traditional engineering approach to the world now carried to lunatic extreme. He views all problems as technical problems, amenable to technical solutions: if "underdeveloped peoples" are starving, let's equip them to eat grass; if their expectations are rising, let's implement "wish evaporation." He's task-oriented, little interested in the larger context; if the problem is "highly technical and complex and interesting," he's excited, and nothing else matters. "Function is the cry." But if he feels threatened, the chief engineer can become quite moralistic, blaming "irresponsible victims" and bragging of his "new moral tool" on computer punched cards. His long list of weapons near the end is at once comic and terrifying, as is the scene of a roomful of engineers with the know-how to kill millions "making calculations . . . drinking beer, throwing bread" and, of course, suffering the consequences of their own ingenious invention, the secret word that fractures bones. Software Man, at least at first, seems quite different; he says the war is "wrong." But by the end (as the pronouns in the last paragraph reveal), he's been won over to the chief engineer's point of view. The year the story was published, the fiendishness of the weapons, the "hut-shrinking chemical" and other references to peasant societies, the amoral technical support for an immoral war — all these suggest that Barthelme was quite aware of the war in Vietnam.

Margaret Drabble, "The Gifts of War"

A richly layered story, "The Gifts of War" is not solely about war or its effects, despite its title. It is set during the late 1960s during a time of antiwar protests in London fueled by discontent over the Vietnam War, and there are memories of World War II in the bombed-out working-class neighborhood the story's protagonist lives in and travels through to reach the department store downtown where she plans to buy her eight-year-old son a birthday present. What the child wants is something called the Desperado Destruction Machine and because he wants it, and because his mother loves him well, that's what she plans to buy with her painfully saved shillings. Not that she has ever considered the political and psychological implications of buying war toys and giving them to children. This is where the second major character, a young woman protester, comes in. Frances is there to help her boyfriend Michael demonstrate against the war, and between the well-meaning two of them, they devastate this unnamed mother's day. The themes concerning war mingle in this story with: 1) explorations of motherhood and its power of salvation for the protagonist of the story; 2) male/female relations in the protagonist's marriage and in the liaison between the protestors, Frances and Michael; 3) generational differences in the perspectives of the two women who alternate narrating the story. "The Gifts of War" therefore might work with selections in Growing Up and Growing Older and in Women and Men and, because it is in part about a demonstration, with some selections in Varieties of Protest.

POETRY

Wilfred Owen, "Dulce Et Decorum Est"

The speaker, addressing a patriotic and probably older "friend," counterposes physical details, the actuality of war, to the abstract lofty sentiments of the Latin quote. While mostly determinedly realistic, the speaker's descriptions (e.g. lines 13 and 14) are also surreal; we get the nightmarish mood as well as the bloody details of combat. There's much irony in the poem — in the comparison of young soldiers to "old beggars" and to "hags"; in the comparison of the face of the innocent dying man to "a devil's sick of sin"; in the title, of course; and in the rhyming, at the end, of "glory" and "mori." The man dies over and over again, in "all my dreams," the speaker says, suggesting that this is but one victim of many and that even those who are unhurt physically continue to suffer psychologically.

Carmen Tafolla, "How Shall I Tell You?"

A sonnet variation — 16 lines instead of the usual 14 — "How Shall I Tell You?" has a lovely traditional lyric sound, in part because of the regular rhyme scheme. A vision of post-nuclear devastation, sparked for the poet by the Chernobyl incident, the poem could be read alongside the Bradbury, Õta, and perhaps Kaminsky pieces in this section. The speaker of the poem visualizes many of the natural and human phenomena that would be missing for her in such an event, chief and finally among them imagining the disappearance of love, since there would be no one there to love and to declare love in words or touch. And so Tafolla's poem is a love poem as well.

Bob Dylan, song: "With God on Our Side"

This antiwar ballad recounts U.S. history through its battles, beginning with those against Native Americans and continuing through the Spanish-American War, the Civil War, the First and Second World Wars, the Cold War, and moving into the speaker's fear of a planet-wide nuclear war. The speaker takes an ostensibly naive stand: history books gave us a particular view of these wars, justifying them because Americans are God's people, God is on our side, ours is not to question why. By the fourth stanza and the First World War, the speaker begins to be confused ("The reason for fighting/I never got straight"), and the ease with which politicians turn enemies into friends after the Second World War ("The Germans now too/Have God on their side") bewilders him. Like Wilfred Owen's "Dulce Et Decorum Est," this song questions the easy patriotic slogans on which we are raised. You might ask students to list a number of such slogans and consider them in relation to real life.

Denise Levertov, "Life at War"

See the brief discussion in "Literature and the Writing Process." "Life at War" is from Levertov's collection The Sorrow Dance, which contains several other anti-Vietnam War poems. The poem's effectiveness is in part based on the vivid contrast between the creative sensitive potential of "delicate Man" and the horrors to which he turns "with mere regret." The speaker's outrage at this spoilage of human potential comes through quite clearly in the poem. Her argument is that while we are perpetrating or supporting or even just passively accepting these horrors, we cannot live in uncomplicated joy or love — if we know that this is happening. "Life at War," like many of Levertov's poems, assumes knowledge and intelligence as central to human existence. What does she mean at the end of the poem by "the deep intelligence [of] living at peace"? See also "What Were They Like?" in this section.

Margaret Atwood, "At first I was given centuries"

The "I" in this poem, of course, is not a single individual but a composite of all the women, through history, left behind waiting for men to return from war. Once students realize this, they should enjoy trying to puzzle out the historical period or kind of war each stanza alludes to. (Some key clues: "jangled," "failed," "sunburn," "twenty years," "my factory overalls," "only seconds," "the street.") It's worth asking students to characterize the speaker and her evolving attitude toward her plight as fully as possible: she "was given" centuries; she finds him "insufferable"; it was three weeks before she "could start regretting"; etc. Note that there is no period at the end of the poem.

e.e. cummings, "next to of course god america i"

Cummings has condensed to its essence the typical politician's July 4th or Memorial Day or monument dedication speech. Even students most deadened by the dishonesty and banality of the utterances of most contemporary American politicians should awaken to cummings's satire. Truncated and run together, the patriotic phrases are revealed as the buzz words that they are for the speechmaker. But his speech is not empty of content, as phrases like "these heroic happy dead" and "they did not stop to think" reveal; this is the kind of talk that helps push people into war. The last line undercuts any credibility the speechmaker might still have; that he drank "rapidly" that glass of water could suggest that even he knows something's wrong. This poem might be read with Wilfred Owen's "Dulce et Decorum Est" or with an excerpt from the newspaper transcript of a recent speech by a major politician.

Carolyn Forché, "The Colonel"

The opening sentence and the flat tone throughout suggest this is the testimony of someone still shocked by what she has seen. The juxtaposition of ordinary details (the newspaper, the dogs, the daughter filing her nails) with signs of brutality (the broken bottles in the wall, the sack of human ears) is chilling, as is the surreal image of the moon swinging "bare on its black cord," suggesting a hanging. The colonel's veneer of culture, politeness, refinement is quite thin; there is good wine and a gold bell for gently calling the maid, but he tells the parrot to "shut up" and he soon explodes in anger at his guests. He hopes to charm them, and needs to, since they probably have connections with human rights investigators ("your people") who can give him bad publicity abroad; but he's used to getting his way more directly, as the ears indicate. The colonel is part of a tiny, wealthy elite living luxuriously at the expense of a desperately poor and no doubt resentful populace (hence those walls around the house) whom they repress mercilessly. A very significant detail in the poem is that cop show "in English" on the television: at Washington D.C.'s International Police Academy and elsewhere, the U.S. government trained many men like the colonel in methods of 'keeping order,' and it sent vast sums of money to El Salvador to support the government they dominate. But the poem ends on a small note of hope: some ears are "pressed to the ground," listening perhaps for distant rumblings of change.

Muriel Rukeyser, "Waking This Morning"

You could ask students to look up "violent," and perhaps also "peace" and "wild." And also to consider what the speaker means by "touch" and "anti-touch." Throughout Rukeyser's work (see the several other poems by her included in the anthology), a formidable intellectuality combines with a strong sensuality and a belief in commitment that is passionate, not pallid. So for the speaker of this poem, peace is strong and good is wild, poems are touch poems, the universe is breathing. Violent means here not only hurting others, which she will avoid by trying to be non-violent; violent also implies passionate, possessed of strong feelings, which the speaker of the poem and the day she wakes to both possess.

Sappho, "To an army wife, in Sardis"

A graceful tribute to an absent friend or perhaps one of Sappho's students, the poem moves between the glories of war and splendid trappings of military life and the personal and individual claims we have on each other. So on the one hand are the swift oars of our fleet and on the other whatever one loves is "the finest/sight on dark earth"; on the one hand we have the heroic struggle and fall of Troy, on the other hand Helen who, "warped to his will," left her own child for him; on the one hand to see Anactoria's eyes would move Sappho more than, on the other hand, "the glitter of Lydian horse." The poem sets up quite clearly a hierarchy of values and uses those to very gently chide Anactoria for choosing to leave Sappho and to go with her army husband.

Richard Lovelace, "To Lucasta, Going to the Wars"

Here is the traditional identification of war with honor. But the usual opposition between war and love is undercut, as the speaker, in the second stanza, describes war in the language of love. His love for Lucasta is pure ("the nunnery/Of thy chaste breast"), while the language of the second stanza suggests something more carnal, as well as violent. But his motive, the third stanza tells her, is simply "honor." Does he protest too much?

John Milton, "On the Late Massacre in Piemont"

What is the tone of this poem? The speaker makes three main requests: "Avenge . . ."; "Forget not . . ."; and "that from these may grow/A hundredfold, who . . ./Early may fly the Babylonian woe." Are these just rhetorical stances? Which does the speaker want most? Why is this description of a massacre cast in the form of a prayer? Why a sonnet?

Alfred Lord Tennyson,
"The Charge of the Light Brigade"

When one of us was a kid, she used to think this poem was about an electrical workers union, but in fact it is a poem celebrating heroism in the traditional sense, in which a group of men on horseback, flashing sabers, ride into cannon fire and get decimated. In spite of the fact that

Some one had blunder'd.
Theirs not to make reply,
Theirs not to reason why,
Theirs but to do and die.

This poem, with its unquestioning adherence to authority, can be set next to Bob Dylan's "With God On Our Side" and the section in Judy Grahn's long poem "A Woman Is Talking To Death ("Varieties of Protest") in which a company of soldiers, following orders, continue to get into defective landing boats that immediately sink. "The Charge of the Light Brigade" could provoke a discussion of our notions of heroism. To what extent have these changed since Tennyson published this poem in 1854; to what extent do they linger on?

Rudyard Kipling, "Tommy"

We are shown the situation of the soldier in a standing army during peace time. The first two stanzas each give us an everyday situation where "Tommy" is discriminated against and the refrain demonstrates how everyone changes their tune during war time. Stanzas 3, 4, & 5 construct an argument for accepting soldiers, even when they aren't "plaster saints." What are the assumptions civilians make about the soldiers? The poem could initiate a debate over about the need for a standing army (or military) and how military enlistees and career people are thought of and treated today in this country. In practice, in this country anyway, the military is almost a separate culture inside the larger culture —the government provides for the economic, medical, social, cultural needs of military people and their families and keeps them somewhat isolated from civilians. Is that a good idea?

Walt Whitman, "The Dying Veteran"

We find this a fairly convincing "pro-war" poem; Whitman parenthetically remarks that it might offend us. What does the dying veteran dislike about the present age? What are the components of his revolutionary war experience that he fondly remembers and sees as the high point of his life? What the war experience sometimes provides for young men might be a question students would like to discuss; an experience of male bonding and the chance to get away from home are two mundane but compelling aspects of that experience.

Rupert Brooke, "The Soldier"

Brooke fought at Antwerp in 1914 and died in April 1915 fighting on the Mediterranean coast. He was buried in Scyros, in "a foreign field/That is forever England." "The Soldier" is one of a group of sonnets he wrote in 1914. It is a hybrid of English sonnet, with the abab cdcd rhyme scheme of the first two quatrains, and Italian sonnet, with the efgefg rhyme scheme of the closing sestet. The first eight lines deal with the body, the last six with the heart or soul of this soldier, killed far away from his native England. This is an appealing, even sweet poem about war. Do students see it as a patriotic poem? What are the words, phrases, lines that make it patriotic?

Margaret Sackville, "Nostra Culpa"

This poem asserts, or implies, a number of things students may wish to discuss: that women know "the worth/Of life," and men don't; that men are warmakers and women can and should be peacemakers; that had they not been silent, women could have prevented or stopped the war; that women, because of their silence, bear responsibility for the deaths of those who fell in the war — "We mothers and we murderers of mankind."

Amy Lowell, "Patterns"

The patterns of the speaker's constricting clothing, the formal 18th-century garden, the rigid social conventions, and the "pattern called war" are all counterposed to what is natural. The speaker had hoped that her and her fiancé's passion would break them out of civilization's imprisoning patterns, but now that he ("the man who should loose me") is dead, she feels condemned forever. Frustrated and angry, she defies decorum and swears in the last line. Students should be interested in discussing what connections there might be between social rigidity and war.

Marina Tsvetayeva, "A White Low Sun"

In this World War I poem by a Russian poet, the perspective is female and civilian. Why does the speaker say, "It's soldiers who sing these days"? (See Whitman's "The Dying Veteran.") What is the experience of civilians in wartime, especially when the war is on their own land? How does that differ from the experience of those who are actively engaged in fighting? Notice the images; how do they, together, create a mood, and what is that mood?

Siegfried Sassoon, "Does it Matter?"

The heavy irony that runs through this poem never becomes overbearing, in part because of Sassoon's carefully controlled diction: "need not," "gobble," "splendid," and so on. You might ask students why he chose each of these over possible alternatives. Ask also why they think he chose the meter and rhyme scheme he did. This poem might be read alongside Margaret Sackville's "Nostra Culpa."

William Butler Yeats, "An Irish Airman Foresees His Death"

Why does this airman, probably a young man, go to war? In the first eight lines of this sonnet, the speaker lists the reasons why he did not enlist. What are they? Then in the last six lines, he gives us his actual motivation — "a lonely impulse of delight." How does this differ from the positive aspects of war that Whitman's dying veteran remembers? You might also look at Brooks's "the sonnet-ballad."

Alice Dunbar-Nelson, "I Sit and Sew"

Unlike the collective voice of women left behind during war that speaks with growing resignation in Margaret Atwood's poem "At first I was given centuries," the speaker in "I Sit and Sew" is increasingly frustrated that she can't somehow actively help the men who are suffering on the battlefield. The intense descriptions of war's brutality — "holocaust of hell"; "writhing grotesque things/Once men" — suggest that perhaps she'd once served as a nurse during war. But now (too old?) she's stuck at home, "beneath my homely thatch," and can only dream of the horrors and of helping. Seemingly trapped in the traditionally female activity of sewing (for the soldiers?) and in a traditionally female passivity, she feels helpless to do anything about "That pageant terrible" — though there's a hint in the change from statement to question in the third stanza's last line that she may finally do something more than sit and sew. Alice Dunbar-Nelson was a longtime activist for African American rights and for world peace. "Dunbar" comes from her first husband, poet Paul Laurence Dunbar.

e.e. cummings, "my sweet old etcetera"

What are the attitudes of the speaker's aunt, sister, mother, and father towards the war? How does "etcetera" deflate each? How does the effect of "etcetera" change as we get to "self etcetera," "mud et/cetera," "dreaming,/etcetera," and "your Etcetera"? What is the effect of an antiwar poem that seems so light and good-natured?

Federico García Lorca, "Ballad of the Spanish Civil Guard"

A poem from the Spanish Civil War, during which many Americans enlisted in International Brigades to oppose the fascist rebellion against Spain's republican government. Lorca himself was executed by Franco's soldiers in 1936. One of the great Spanish poets of the twentieth century, Lorca was influenced by the Surrealist Movement, which can be seen in his use of imagery in this poem; it goes beneath realism to pull evocative images out of the subconscious and to juxtapose images to shock the reader into a new awareness. "They have, and so they never weep,/Skulls of lead/With patent leather souls" or "City of grief and of musk/with towers of cinnamon." As well as considering the images, ask students what is literally happening in the poem. See also Chilean poet Pablo Neruda's "Ode to Federico García Lorca" in "Varieties of Protest."

Bertolt Brecht, "From a German War Primer"

We tend to think of war (at least before the Vietnam War) as unifying a nation, uniting citizens in a common struggle against an external enemy. Brecht's uncompromising aphorisms look at war from the point of view of "the lowly" and proclaim the real enemy to be their class enemy, "THOSE AT THE TOP." Is Brecht the pessimist and cynic much of this poem might suggest, or is there, in the last stanzas, an optimistic faith in humanity's potential? And why has Brecht written a "primer"?

Babette Deutsch, "Dawn in Wartime"

What is the specific setting of this World War II poem and what is the situation of the speaker (or the person the speaker observes)? Deutsch uses here, as writers about war often do, the technique of contrast between peace and violence. Here the violence is implied in lines 4 - 8 and the rest of the poem is a marvel of soul lifting peace and natural beauty. As well as sight, the sense of touch or texture is evoked strongly in this poem. You could ask students to list the images of touch (e.g., "giant comber, soft as roses" vs. "cold cliffs") and how the poet creates a mood through imagery.

H.D. (Hilda Doolittle), from The Walls Do Not Fall

The Walls Do Not Fall is the first volume of H.D.'s World War II trilogy. Each of the three volumes contains a sequence of poems. We have included here four of the poems from The Walls Do Not Fall, the first and the last (43) as well as two of the more accessible poems in the volume.

In poem 1, ask students to note the images of bombed out houses and the parallels between the architectural ruins and the human body. Also note the title of the poem in this context and the survival of Spirit. Finally, the questioning. "What saved us? What for?" In poem 14, why (given poem 1) does the speaker call us "twice- born"? What is the extended image in this poem; what are human beings compared to: "dragging the forlorn husk of self after us" and "we have not crawled so very far/up our individual grass- blade." What are the implications of this comparison, of our limitations? Is the tone critical? In poem 33, she suggests in the first two stanzas what we should do and in stanzas three to six what we ought not to do in these post war times. The last poem of the volume (43) goes back to the title and the image of the ruined, bomb torn houses of poem 1. What is the situation of the "we" of the poem, in a world where "even the air is independable"? Nothing in this world can be counted on; the old certainties have vanished; we are (as in poem 14) bewildered, groping along in a "blind fog," voyagers without a map. Still, as in the first poem, there is some hope in the human spirit. "Possibly we will reach haven/heaven."

Randall Jarrell, "The Death of the Ball Turret Gunner"

Childhood and adolescence are collapsed into an instant as the speaker moves from birth to possession by "the State," from his mother's womb to the womb-like ball turret in the belly of a war plane. He wakes into a "nightmare" and is killed before he's had a chance to live.

Ultimately anonymous and replaceable, he's washed out with a hose as the plane is made ready for the next gunner.

Gwendolyn Brooks, "the white troops had their orders but the Negroes looked like men"

This is a sonnet, like Brooks's "sonnet ballad," also in this section. Students may not realize that the U.S. army that fought against the racist Nazis in World War II was thoroughly segregated. The white troops in Brooks's poem had been prepared by their superiors for an encounter with black soldiers, told to cast a cold eye on them. But faced with fellow human beings, "Negroes [who] looked like men," the white troops were "perplexed"; their indoctrination began failing. Part of the psychology of war is to employ xenophobia, to divide the world into us and other, other being those you are fighting. Brooks suggests the white troops found it too complicated to have yet another set of categories of Other ("a box for dark men and a box for Other/would often find the contents had been scrambled.") For, as the last two lines suggest, racism is not natural.

Claude McKay, "Look Within"

On a different and angrier note than Brooks in "the white troops . . . ", McKay points out the outrage of a country fighting fascism in Europe and Asia while perpetuating racism at home. How does McKay use Biblical references to construct his argument? See also Owen Dodson's "Black Mother Praying."

Henry Reed, "Naming of Parts"

The young soldier being subjected to a dull lecture on the parts of the gun he'll soon have to use finds his mind drifting (in the later part of each stanza) towards the garden's beauty and towards sex. Double meanings and contrasts (nature vs. mechanism, life vs. death, etc.)

abound, as these thoughts unfold in the shadow of a war that will soon put a quick end to many young lives. The images of sexuality here offer a chance to link this poem to issues of sexism explored more fully in the "Women and Men" section.

Owen Dodson, "Black Mother Praying"

Like Gwendolyn Brooks's poem "the white troops had their orders but the Negroes looked like men" (see comments there), this poem dramatizes the bitter irony of racism in a nation at war against Hitler. Dodson emphasizes the sacrifices black people (like this mother and her family) are making and the treatment they are getting in return. Why has Dodson chosen not to write in "Standard" English? Why has he chosen the form of a prayer? From the text, can we tell whether he is writing primarily for black or for white readers?

Gwendolyn Brooks, "the sonnet-ballad"

Here's the seductiveness of war for a young man — but as seen by the young woman he's left behind. The poem might be read along with Margaret Atwood's "At first I was given centuries." And it offers an interesting contrast to Richard Lovelace's "To Lucasta, Going to the Wars"; there, too, war is a "new mistress," but Lovelace's speaker denies what Brooks's asserts: that to pursue her is to be "untrue."

Why does Brooks name this a ballad as well as a sonnet? How are war and death seen by the female speaker of the poem? Along with several other poems in this section — Whitman, "The Dying Veteran"; Tennyson, "Charge of the Light Brigade"; Yeats, "An Irish Airman Foresees His Death" — this one explores (though from a female rather than a male perspective) the lure of war. What are the personal and psychological attractions of war? And are these specific to men? And are they innate or learned?

Yevgeny Yevtushenko, "The Companion"

Written by one of the Soviet Union's best poets, "The Companion" is set during World War II and focuses on two children who suddenly find themselves alone during an attack, cut off from the adults who have been taking care of them. Whose is the point of view in the poem? What does the speaker learn? How does Yevtushenko make this into a charming and moving encounter? How does he combine humor with horror? How are the images of shoes central to the poem?

Robert Lowell, "For the Union Dead"

Lowell mingles his feelings about the loss of the world of his childhood (and its landmarks) with what he sees as the decline and decay of American culture and values. The heroic sacrifice of Colonel Shaw and his regiment have given way to selfishness, ugliness, materialism — "a savage servility/slides by on grease." The Civil War monument offers an image of pure heroism and "sticks like a fishbone" in the throat of a city bent on baser pursuits. The only symbol of war since Colonel Shaw's war is the photograph of Hiroshima in a tasteless advertisement for a Mosler safe (and it's worth asking students to explore all the implications of this image). "For the Union Dead" might be contrasted with Wilfred Owen's "Dulce Et Decorum Est," which also begins with a patriotic epigraph.

Denise Levertov, "What Were They Like?"

Many who opposed the Vietnam war called it "genocidal" and Levertov, writing before the war even reached its peak, imagines in this poem that genocide has been completed. Ask students to characterize, in a word or phrase, Vietnamese culture as Levertov depicts it. How, by implication, is she characterizing those who have destroyed it? What are the possible identities (soldier? anthropologist? etc.) for each speaker? What does Levertov achieve by using a question and answer format? By asking all the questions before answering any of them?

Nguyen Lam Son, "Can Tho"

After the French occupiers were defeated at Dienbienphu in 1954, an agreement signed in Geneva temporarily divided Vietnam in two, the northern part to be controlled by the Viet Minh, led by Ho Chi Minh, the southern part to be controlled by the French. Elections to choose a government of a united Vietnam were to be held in 1956, but the United States (which by 1954 had been paying 78% of France's war costs) installed Ngo Dinh Diem in the South and urged him to refuse to participate in elections. (Most historians agree that Ho Chi Minh would have been elected president.) Opposition to Diem grew in the South and in 1960 the National Liberation Front was formed. The Communist government in the North gave aid to the NLF, but there was no significant regular North Vietnamese troop presence in the South until well after major U.S. troop deployment there. As part of its effort to justify its intervention in Vietnam, the United States government insisted on portraying the civil war in the South as an invasion from the North. This poem comes from captured "North Vietnamese documents," but in all probability its author never left the South. "Ca Mau" Peninsula is at the extreme southern end of Vietnam.

Langston Hughes, "Without Benefit of Declaration"

Who is the poem addressed to and where does that change? Note Hughes's images — the steel winds, the lead rain, and "hidden from the sky." Like a number of the poems in this section, "Without Benefit of Declaration" questions the unquestioning acceptance by individuals (usually young men) of a call to war. "Don't ask me why./Just go ahead and die."

Anonymous, "Americans Are Not Beautiful"

There was much support in Saigon for the U.S. war effort — particularly among those who made a living off the billions of dollars that flowed in — and along with this support came enthusiasm for American mass culture, styles, physical appearance, and so on. But the young speaker in this poem sees through it all, sees the destruction the American invasion has wrought. Virtually every American film or literary work about the Vietnam war — no matter how critical it is of the war — tells its story from an American point of view. This poem offers a Vietnamese point of view. Its assumption of Vietnamese physical characteristics as the norm provides an interesting commentary on the racist aspects of a war in a land of people that Americans called "gooks." To prepare students to hear that "Americans are not beautiful," you might first discuss Denise Levertov's poem "What Were They Like?"

Judy Grahn, "Vietnamese woman speaking to an American soldier"

Written from a Vietnamese woman's perspective, the poem connects sex and war, both realistically (since the women of an occupied country are, unfortunately, usually sexually available to the occupying soldiers) and metaphorically, as images of violence merge, in the middle of the poem, with the sexuality. This poem brings up again, as do several of the poems in this section, the plight of civilians in a war zone. And it explores a theme several other poems here take up — the bewilderment over what all this active violence is about and for.

Carolyn Forché, "The Visitor"

See also Forché's "The Colonel" in this section. While "The Colonel" focuses on a member of the military dictatorship in El Salvador, "The Visitor" presents a prisoner of that regime. The visitor is presumably the poet/observer (as in "The Colonel") trying to capture and present a situation vividly and also to comment on it, as she does in the last and set off line: "There is nothing one man will not do to another." How does Forché select and present images to give us a portrait of this prisoner? What about the tension, here and in "The Colonel," between the speaker's reportorial stance and her emotional response to what she is observing? This is also an issue in Yōko Ōta's story, "Fireflies."

Joy Harjo, "Resurrection"

In July 1979, a revolutionary movement led by the Sandinista National Liberation Front overthrew the failing dictatorship of Anastasio Somoza. By 1981, the United States was organizing and funding ex-somocistas to overthrow the new government of Nicaragua. The Sandinistas enjoyed widespread support and the Contras, as their armed opponents were called, sought to weaken the government by terrorizing its supporters and targeting the institutions it was building up: agricultural cooperatives, schools, health centers. Contras operated freely in Honduras and used it as a base from which to launch attacks on northern Nicaragua; Estelí, near the border, was especially vulnerable. In the poem, daily life in this town is lived in the shadow of the Contra war. People try to carry on with their lives, but at any moment, "the night could change." The dead are a constant presence, as are the wounded; all long for resurrection.

Otto Orban, "Chile"

In 1970, despite CIA efforts to help defeat him, Salvador Allende Gossens, of the socialist Popular Unity party, was elected president of Chile. Allende expanded agrarian reform, distributed food to the poor, and nationalized key industries, most notably copper mining. The U.S. government began a program of largely covert efforts to destabilize the Allende government (necessary, Henry Kissinger later said, to save Chile from "the irresponsibility of its own people"). On September 11, 1973, with the help of the CIA, the Chilean military seized power, putting an end to democratic rule in Latin America's oldest democracy. In the wake of the coup, the military junta, led by General Augusto Pinochet Ugarte, began executing activists, intellectuals, and other Allende supporters; estimates run as high as 30,000 killed. Otto Orban's short prose poem dramatizes a moment of this history in the life of one family.

Bella Akhmadulina, "Words Spoken by Pasternak During a Bombing"

Ask students to relate what the literal situation of the poem is. What insights does the speaker of the poem come to about himself in this situation? About his relation to other living things? In the first, fifth, and last stanzas, he refers to himself as a "mountain stone" — what does he mean by this? The poem can be read with Levertov's "Life at War," Tafolla's "How Shall I Tell You?", Yevtushenko's "The Companion," and perhaps Deutsch's "Dawn in Wartime." Ask students to imagine being in a bombing attack. How would they feel and what might they do? Kaminsky's play, In the Traffic of a Targeted City, gives us several examples of what people actually did and/or fantasized doing in such situations.

Bruce Weigl, "Song of Napalm"

A vivid illustration of how the traumatic past intrudes into, intersects with, and overlays a present time in which one might be experiencing joy or contentment. Superimposed on the pasture of horses the speaker and his wife are looking at is the image burned into his mind of a Vietnamese girl running along a road, dying horribly of the napalm that covers her. Unable to banish the image, the speaker tries to change it in imagination, to give her wings to fly away from her pain (and his and his wife's). But that lie doesn't work and in fact there is no getting away from those memories. Weigl's poem is companioned well by Lady Borton's essay "Wars Past and Wars Present."

Dwight Okita, "In Response to Executive Order 9066: ALL AMERICANS OF JAPANESE DESCENT MUST REPORT TO RELOCATION CENTERS"

In 1942, Executive Order 9066 sent over 100,000 Japanese Americans to internment camps, among them Dwight Okita's father and his mother. The fourteen-year-old speaker in the poem appears naively optimistic at the start (so much so that the opening almost seems sarcastic). Despite what her father says, she's determined to grow tomatoes in the camp. Her eager, almost pathetic efforts to be seen as just another typical American teenager like her best friend Denise are thwarted when Denise, newly indoctrinated, accuses her of being a traitor. Now it seems unlikely tomato plants, or anything else, will thrive in the camp. So she gives the seeds to Denise. Only fourteen, she's not entirely demoralized; she still assumes Denise will "miss" her. As distressing as the speaker's eagerness to prove herself an American is the speed with which Denise accepts the lies about her and rejects her.

Margaret Atwood, "The Loneliness of the Military Historian"

Pair this with the other poem we've included by Atwood on war, "At first I was given centuries." The speaker there is also a woman, and one in the more traditional role (like Rukeyser's speaker in "Waiting For Icarus") of the woman who waits while the man (husband, father, son, brother) goes off to war. Here the speaker is a woman academic — a military historian — telling the unpleasant truth about war: that there are no heroes or villains; that brutality, technology, disease, and hunger are more effective than valor or honor or right; that, as she concludes, "for every year of peace there have been four hundred/years of war." In the first two stanzas of the poem, especially the savage second stanza, she challenges the stereotypes of women's proper role regarding war. Having done that, the rest of the poem takes on our assumptions and illusions about war, including the assumption that it's an aberration rather than the normal state of affairs.

Barbara Kingsolver, "Deadline"

The war against Iraq was a hard war to oppose; as the poem says, the polls sang "their opera of assent." But no war is easy to oppose, and the speaker is glad to see a fellow protester "still here," undaunted by the seeming powerlessness of a flickering candlelight vigil against a mighty war machine that can throw a brilliant "liquid sheet" of burning gasoline "wide as the ancient Tigris." The speaker emphasizes the child's beauty, and her vulnerability and preciousness ("It has taken your whole self/to bring her undamaged to this moment"), a mere hint of what will be lost as wanton killing destroys innumerable lives. All the more reason to be one of those "who stood in front of every war," who tried to stop war's progress, who did not give up even though hope was no more than a "carcass." For "a way out" must somehow be found.

DRAMA

Marc Kaminsky, In the Traffic of a Targeted City

Though this play is fairly easy to follow on the page, students will get more out of it if parts or all of it are performed or at least read out loud. In performance, all the characters are played by two actors, a man and a woman. The two settings are New York City in the 1980s and Hiroshima in 1945 just before and after the dropping of the atomic bomb. The actors don kimonos to play the Japanese characters and the male actor an overcoat and hat to play Uncle Max; otherwise they are in jeans and shirts. In a class reading, however, each of these several parts could be given to a different student.

The sections set in Hiroshima are based on diaries of survivors of the atomic bomb. You could discuss the changes in cadence and tone between the New York scenes and the Hiroshima scenes. How well do the New York scenes (Jonah's first long speech on the subway, for example) accurately characterize life in the 80s, especially urban life? What are the specific characteristics that make up the ambiance of the 80s? What is the function of the character of Walkman?

Uncle Max, survivor of the Nazi Holocaust, provides a bridge between Jonah and Joanna's urban 1980s life and the experience of Nakajima and others in Japan in 1945. Uncle Max has three speeches. He is a man who knew something was wrong in Germany but didn't speak, just went along, was put into a concentration camp, and managed to survive. He concludes: "You ask: How could we/go to our deaths like sleepwalkers? But you of all people/should not ask."

The scenes in Hiroshima, perhaps in part because they are based on the words of people who experienced the last days of the war in Japan, the bomb, and especially the aftermath, are the most moving in the play. In Joanna's speech in the persona of a young Japanese girl that begins "Not aware/of what I was doing. . ." note the imagery of shoes and other material objects, the use of time, the baby trying to nurse at her dead mother's breast, the blouse that falls apart.

Does the juxtaposition of scenes between Hiroshima and New York City work for readers? The juxtaposition of horror and humor? You might read this play along with Yōko Ōta's "Fireflies" and Ray Bradbury's "August 2026: There Will Come Soft Rains."

NONFICTION

Black Elk, "The Butchering at Wounded Knee"

When Europeans first arrived in what is now the United States, it was populated by perhaps one million Indians. By 1900, the figure was 300,000. The massacre at Wounded Knee was just about the last battle of the war against the native Americans. Indians had been almost completely confined to reservations by then and they no longer fought back. In the last years of Native American resistance, the Ghost Dance religion grew up; a key belief was that "ghost shirts" could protect those who wore them from the cavalry's bullets. Black Elk's account reveals the importance not only of the land but of ritual in the lives of his people: he puts on his "sacred shirt" and paints his face; he and the others sing a song before attempting to rescue their relatives; and he holds out his "sacred bow," which he believes protects him from bullets, as he rides towards the soldiers. Given the horrors he saw, Black Elk's tone is remarkably (and effectively) flat, his emotion breaking through the surface only near and at the end. This piece might be read along with Louise Erdrich's story, "The Red Convertible." A sense of this history should enrich students' response to that story.

Ron Kovic, from Born on the Fourth of July

When Kovic is wounded, all he wants is "to live," and he feels "tremendous exhilaration" once he thinks he's going to make it. But the worst is still to come; its aftermath, more than war, is hell. His life is one of many "living deaths" that fill the hospital wards. Even the general who mechanically dispenses Purple Hearts and Polaroids is given pause (momentarily) by what he sees. Students may find Kovic's descriptions of enemas and maimed bodies "gross" — but this is what his life consists of in the hospital. He and the others are treated like things; much of his agony comes from his inability to see himself that way. The use of present tense gives certain scenes greater immediacy and also the quality of a recurring nightmare. (There's considerable irony in the last words of the first section: "I leave Vietnam forever.") Perhaps Kovic's use of the third person in the beginning of the second section represents his attempt to get some distance on his own experience as he writes this autobiography. Kovic's book continues after this opening excerpt with a long flashback that details his growing up into a patriotic, athletic, working-class young man; then his enlistment in the Marines; and then basic training. From there, it goes to recount his life after Vietnam: he's put on display at a jingoistic Memorial Day celebration, he tries to find love, he joins Vietnam Veterans Against the War, and he becomes a powerful anti-war speaker and activist. The guilt-ridden references to the "corporal" and the "children" become more frequent and we finally learn that he accidentally killed a fellow soldier in Vietnam and that he and others "shot up" a hut full of children and old men, thinking they were 'the enemy.'

Martin Luther King, Jr., from "A Time to Break Silence"

One way to approach "A Time To Break Silence" is to consider it, formally, as a speech. What characterizes speeches or sermons as a nonfictional prose form (see "How Nonfiction Works")? Clarity, accessibility, repetition, enumeration of points, personalizing of the speaker, direct contact with and address to an audience, rhetorical devices like questions are a few components of effective oral prose that King uses here. Also take a look at King's famous "I Have A Dream" in the "Varieties of Protest" section. You might also place "A Time to Break Silence" in a group of works about the Vietnam War, including Ron Kovic's Born on the Fourth of July. Louise Erdrich's "The Red Convertible," Donald Barthelme's "Report," Denise Levertov's poems "Life at War" and "What Were They Like?", the anonymous "Americans Are Not Beautiful," and Grahn's "Vietnamese woman speaking to an American soldier," all in this section. How does Martin Luther King, Jr.'s position as a Black Civil Rights leader structure his perspective and his argument in this speech? How do his position and perspective as a minister also shape his argument?

Lady Borton, "Wars Past and Wars Present"

Borton watches "boat people" from Vietnam "gripping the cabin roof like bees clinging in layers to the face of a hive." The suffering of people en masse is difficult to comprehend, to relate to, as the simile suggests. But up close, the suffering of individuals victimized by war can be palpable and real. In her effort to "place politics aside and address the continuing human effects of the war," Borton describes the plight of Springtime or Flower or Luon very directly and concretely. But the ultimate causes of their suffering, the "politics" of it all, she conveys more subtly. The juxtaposition, at the start, of Robert's story about "hunting Vietcong," the pleasant restaurant in which he tells it, and the glass crocks containing babies deformed by Agent Orange implies connections between gung-ho U.S. militarism, the comfortable distance of most Americans from the war's destruction, and the effects of that war on the Vietnamese, over two million of whom were killed. Later in the essay, surrounded by supermarket abundance, Borton suddenly remembers starving refugees in Vietnam. The juxtaposition, again, is striking, even horrifying. But are there also connections? Students have no doubt seen, and been moved by, television images of starving Third World children; we have so much and they have so little. You might want to use Borton's essay as an occasion to ask why?

VARIETIES
OF PROTEST

Even if students haven't had any actual experience of political protests, they will probably remember times they engaged in or felt like engaging in individual protest against something they found unfair or unjust: an injustice perpetrated by their parents or by an older sibling, or by people in their peer group, or by some authority figure like a teacher. (Did they ever receive a grade they didn't feel was fair, for example?)

A number of the selections in Varieties of Protest focus on individual protest — on the right and the obligation of an individual to act according to her or his conscience. Thoreau and John Woolman argue this point of view in their nonfiction pieces and Antigone has no choice but to act out of her conscience in Sophocles' play. The concept of integrity recurs in these selections. Harriet Jacobs, like Antigone, has to do what she has to do, likewise Harriet Tubman in Griffin's poem, Smith in Sillitoe's "The Loneliness of the Long-distance Runner," and presumably Melville's Bartleby, though we never see inside that character's head.

The works included here are about modes of protest as well as about issues protested; selections could be grouped either way. Works about individual protests, in addition to the ones mentioned above, include the stories by Cisneros, "Woman Hollering Creek" and Fisher, "A Drop in the Bucket"; Childress's play Florence; poems by Piercy, "What's That Smell in the Kitchen?"; Ginsberg, "America"; Plath, "Daddy"; Grahn, "A Woman is Talking to Death"; Parker, "Where Will You Be?"; Seeger's song, "I'm Gonna Be An Engineer"; and Whitecloud's autobiographical essay, "Blue Winds Dancing." Examples of political demonstrations, group protests, include the stories by McPherson and Gordimer, poems by Dunbar, Margaret Walker, Hogan, and Rich, and Martin Luther King, Jr.'s "I Have A Dream." In addition, a number of pieces consider the consequences and the costs of protest. See our notes in this manual on the additional poems.

You might want to group pieces by issue protested, in which case several of the works included here will each fit with literature in the other sections: Women and Men, Money and Work, Peace and War, and Growing Up and Growing Older. Works about protests by women against the constraints of gender roles include stories by Zoline and Cisneros, Antigone, Jacobs's Incidents in the Life of a Slave Girl, and poems by Griffin, Rich, Plath, Piercy, Carson, and Harjo. These can be grouped with the Brady, Truth, Woolf, Ibsen, Gilman, Grahn, and Erdrich selections in Women and Men. Works involving protests against racism in this section include the Gordimer story, all of the nonfictional prose pieces, and poems by Dunbar, Patterson, and Margaret Walker. They could be grouped with the Ellison, Silko, Baldwin, and Morrison fiction in Growing Up and Growing Older; with Bambara's story "The Lesson," the selection from Angelou's I Know Why the Caged Bird Sings, Hansberry's play A Raisin in the Sun, and poems by Langston Hughes, Jimmy Santiago Baca, and Gwendolyn Brooks in Money and Work; and with King's speech "A Time to Break Silence" and Black Elk's memoir "The Butchering at Wounded Knee" as well as poems by Okita, Dodson, McKay, and Dunbar-Nelson in Peace and War. Protests against economic oppression and class privilege cross race and gender lines. The McPherson, Gordimer, and Sillitoe stories, the Jacobs narrative, and Childress's play Florence have economic oppression as a main component, as do poems by Seeger and Hughes; these might be grouped with selections in Money and Work: the stories by Olsen, Kromer, Bambara, and Walker, the LeSueur and Wright essays, poems by Brecht, Swift, Hardy, Hughes, and Brooks, and Hansberry's play, A Raisin in the Sun. In Growing Up and Growing Older, "A Mistaken Charity" and "Lullaby" concern economic constraint, as do poems by Brooks and Giovanni.

It is probably important to note the way conditions protested against overlap; people often experience some combination of race, ethnic, gender, sexual orientation, age, class, economic, and other oppressions simultaneously. Some students in a classroom might be familiar with one or more of these experiences; others might find it hard to identify with any of them. We have found that a useful exercise is to set up small groups of, say, three students and ask them each to speak briefly in their small group about a personal experience of second-class status in which they felt they were being treated unjustly, were being discriminated against. It is important not to rank oppressions; the point of the exercise is to get people in touch with an experience of oppression and the complex of feelings — humiliation, powerlessness, fear, bewilderment, and anger — that went along with that experience. That way we hope they will be able to approach the literature somewhat from the inside and empathetically. Another focus for class discussion might be the philosophical questions and political strategies that emerge from the readings. The question of tactics — from passive resistance to rioting — and the limits of acting out of one's individual conscience are sure to come up, as well as people's opinions on the various issues protested. Trying to get students to talk about what they would do in a given situation that a literary text brings up is usually a good way into a lively class discussion.

FICTION

Herman Melville, "Bartleby, the Scrivener"

See comments in the preface to this section. "Bartleby, the Scrivener" was published in Melville's collection of stories, The Piazza Tales, which also included "Benito Cereno" and "The Encantadas." The stories were written between Moby Dick and The Confidence Man. What characterizes all of these is a dark ambiguity. As in The Confidence Man and the later "Billy Budd," here in "Bartleby, the Scrivener" the ambiguity is located in the title character, an office clerk who appears mysteriously and whose behavior baffles his boss and co-workers. "Bartleby" is also similar to The Confidence Man and "Billy Budd" in that the point of view is located not in the title character but in one or several other characters, who attempt to make sense of the central figure. Here the first person narrator is Bartleby's employer. As with Captain Vere in "Billy Budd," we see and try to make sense of the title character through the point of view of another character. How does this limit and shape our vision of Bartleby? What is it about Bartleby's manner and his "I would prefer not to" that stymies the narrator? How does the particular character of the narrator, who introduces himself by remarking on his profound conviction that the easiest way of life is the best, provide for this bewildered response to Bartleby's resistance? Beyond the story itself, you might discuss passive resistance as a mode of protest, in political action and in daily life. When does it work and when does it not? To be effective, it seems to assume a certain ethical sense in either the legal system or the individuals protested against; what can happen when that ethical sense is missing?

Pamela Zoline, "The Heat Death of the Universe"

See comments in the preface. Section 26, "Light and Cleaning Up the Living Room," presents two images — of Sarah trapped like an insect fossilized in amber and of the chaos that would result if she quit cleaning and ordered the house on Dada principles. These images, which provide a subversive undercurrent in the story, work well with Adrienne Rich's "The Trees" and with Marge Piercy's more direct "What's That Smell in the Kitchen?" as examples of women's anger about being trapped in roles that limit development of their potential.

As a science fiction story, "The Heat Death of the Universe" could be paired with Bradbury's "August 2026: There Will Come Soft Rains," both using science — Bradbury's applied and Zoline's theoretical — and, formally, both using time devices to count down toward some (destructive?) resolution. Zoline's "resolution" is the more ambiguous and students often focus on the ending of the story — has Sarah finally flipped out entirely? — so the writing exercise we suggest in which students add another numbered paragraph and extrapolate what happens next is useful. In terms of whether Sarah has had a breakdown or a breakthrough, this is a good story to pair with Charlotte Perkins Gilman's "The Yellow Wallpaper" (in "Women and Men") noting that one is from an earlier phase of feminism in this country. Beyond the differences in technology and superficial elements of lifestyle, how similar are the situations of these two women? How much hope we see for Sarah in part depends on whether we feel she is indeed in a closed (isolated) system. See sections 13, 19, and 54. Before her final breakthrough/breakdown, there are two earlier incidents (see 18, about dying her hair, and 37, the wonderful scene in the supermarket). Sarah is wound up very tight.

James Alan McPherson, "A Loaf of Bread"

The omniscient, rather aloof, mildly amused narrator seems to give roughly equal time to Green's and Reed's points of view, to the arguments of the grocer and the arguments of the protestors. Green and Reed have irreconcilable perspectives, rooted in their respective experiences; they speak different languages, Green the language of accounting and Reed the language of religion; neither seems capable of seeing the other as that other sees himself. In each family, the wife, not trapped in pride and bitterness like her husband is, seems primarily concerned with the impact of the conflict on family life. But the situation is hardly symmetrical. Green owns three stores, while Reed works on an assembly line; Reed, as he puts it, couldn't afford the shoes Green wants him to put himself in. The poor black protesters can be briefly "empowered" by their protest because they have so little power to start with. Green insists he is "not an evil man." You might ask students if they agree. Is Green the problem, or is it the rules (comically expounded by Thomas, the "college graduate") that society has given him to play by? Can he avoid individual responsibility that easily? At the end, it may seem that Reed is simply too proud to accept the restitution Green has made; but the free-for-all Green set his customers up for took away the dignity they had achieved as protesters. The grocer may now be "Free! Free! Free!" but they're still stuck in the same place.

Sandra Cisneros, "Woman Hollering Creek"

". . .to suffer for love is good. The pain all sweet somehow. In the end." So runs the message of the telenovelas young Cleófilas watches. But as Juan Pedro's wife, she suffers more and more, and whatever love there might once have been is killed. Students may be impatient with the protagonist's passivity and not understand why she doesn't simply pick up and leave. So it's worth encouraging them to spell out all the things that might be standing in her way, not only the more obvious barriers — she is in the middle of nowhere, can't drive, doesn't speak English, has no one to help her, and knows she'll be hurt even more if caught fleeing — but also the somewhat less obvious barriers, her need not to 'fail' at being a wife, the shame she fears if she returns home, a certain trained passivity, and so on. She's been taught to define herself and value herself only in relation to a man, once her father, perhaps, now her husband, not unlike Soledad and, especially, Dolores, her neighbors who continue to do so even though the men are gone. So it's only by chance that Cleófilas gets help, from Graciela, and then from Felice (a significant name, like many others in the story). Felice shows Cleófilas possibilities she could barely imagine before — a woman living without a husband, driving a pickup, her own pickup; a woman's holler not of "pain or rage" but of freedom and joy and defiance.

Nadine Gordimer, "Something for the Time Being"

There are hints throughout the story of what South Africa is like, but you might want to ask students what they know, and jointly sketch out the picture: apartheid laws, the economic situation of the black majority, arbitrary arrests, etc. Madge Chadders has always responded to all this in a deeply human way; she feels "disgust" at injustice and she protests in whatever way is available to her. "Enchanted" by Madge, William seems to have come to share her political views, in fact, as she sees it, taken them further, by building a philosophical framework to support them and by using his power as a "wealthy businessman" to make things happen. William thinks he can compartmentalize his politics. He can believe in "absolute personal freedom," dislike apartheid, even help with a scheme to "get Africans some economic power." But as a factory owner, he is just that; his central aim, like that of his partner, is to "sell more earth-moving gear." He can tell Daniel Mngoma to remove his ANC button and can spout cant about "a stable, satisfied black labour force." There are hints of the thinness of his progressive veneer before the fight with Madge over the button (you might ask students what they are), but it's only then that she starts "to get to know " her husband. The conflict between Daniel and Ella is also over politics and protest. She knows as well as he does how badly their people are suffering, but she doesn't share his intense involvement in the movement for change. At the end, he's running off to a meeting while she's sewing a dress for their daughter (who has to live a day's train ride away); he wants to transform the world, while she just wants desperately to hold on to what little they have; he's ready to rot in prison contemplating a future when black people will have "everything" they need, while she's trying to find her family "something" for the time being. The juxtaposition of these two marital conflicts, which have certain elements in common, dramatizes the vast differences between the lives of black and white South Africans.

Dorothy Canfield Fisher, "A Drop in the Bucket"

Much of the charm and humor of this story lie in the affectionate portrayal of the two main characters. Though their differences are a source of comedy early on, Cousin Tryphena and Jombatiste are similar in that the heart of neither one has hardened. Jombatiste insists that "any man who could not earn a good living for his family [has] a moral right to shoot a millionaire" and he also protests cruelty to rabbits — both positions come from the same impulse, for "his ardent old heart was evidently as tender as it was hot." He loves children and he loves "inflammatory magazines." Cousin Tryphena, of course, knows nothing of the world, but once she hears about and then sees its injustices, she too aches to do something. Her naiveté and earnestness throw into relief the indifference of everyone else; that they think her crazy indicates how blind (perhaps willfully) they are. The story is very much about education. We see the failures, the successes, and the comedy of Jombatiste's efforts to educate Cousin Tryphena and we see the education of the narrator, as she moves from affectionate amusement at Tryphena to genuine respect for this "heroic old cousin." You might ask students how they would respond to someone like Tryphena today? In a cynical society, does uncorrupted virtue seem lunatic?

Alan Sillitoe, "The Loneliness of the Long-distance Runner"

Sillitoe's choice of first person narration puts us firmly into Smith's perspective and his view of the British class system. Smith is not only a working-class adolescent, but a self admitted thief and proud of it. The Us and Them he describes, the Outlaws and the Inlaws, are seen from the point of view of a convicted thief in a reform school. Sillitoe deliberately sets up an ethical/political dilemma for his readers because, on one level, Smith's class analysis is a justification for his continuing in his life as a criminal. And Sillitoe further outrages middle-class sensibilities with the scene at the beginning of section II showing how Smith's family lived when they got the insurance money from his father's death. Sillitoe wants us finally to identify with Smith's point of view, but he takes us through a layer of easy identification and then a layer of resistance based on the value system most readers have before we get to the deeper understanding of Smith's rebellion. Sillitoe challenges our notions of integrity and of honesty. Why is the choice Smith makes at the end the most honest choice he can make? And how does this choice, made in the process of running the race, allow him to finally come to the insight and understanding about the integrity of his father's death that he needs in order to be a whole person?

The story is in three sections. The first takes us on a practice run and introduces the Us and Them theme (see especially the picnic scene), the conflict in the form of the coming competition, and the running itself, which increasingly becomes a symbol for living. The second section is a flashback to the robbery and subsequent events up to the time Smith is caught. (The events leading up to the robbery — his father's death, the insurance money and how happy they were when they didn't have to hunt for a job — are worth focusing on.) The third section is the race itself; the form returns to the meditative mode of the first section; the carrot of class mobility through athletic success is dangled in front of Smith here but he's already made his decision. Why does he cry toward the end of the race? In what ways does Smith win through losing? How hard is it to lose something you know you can win?

POETRY

Paul Laurence Dunbar, "We Wear the Mask"

More recent black writers might urge black readers to tear off the mask, but to Dunbar the mask seemed an inescapable fact of life: people with "tortured souls" smiled and grinned as a survival tactic. Is wearing the mask (as Dunbar describes it) a form of protest, or does it simply represent the inability to protest? If students have already read Ralph Ellison's "Battle Royal" (in the "Growing Up and Growing Older" section), they might take another look at its second paragraph along with this poem.

Margaret Walker, "For My People"

Whitmanesque long lines, lists, repetition give energy and momentum to this protest and celebration. Its subject is immense but the poem never seems abstract. It sweeps through the North and the South, the past, the present, and the future; it connects the speaker's own life to the life of her people. It begins by telling of singing and praying and ends with a call to action. The new world it calls for "will hold all the people, all the faces, all the adams and eves and their countless generations" — but it will not come easily.

Susan Griffin, "I Like to Think of Harriet Tubman"

See also Griffin's poem, "This Is the Story of the Day in the Life of a Woman Trying" (in "Money and Work"). Griffin, like poets Judy Grahn and Pat Parker also included in this section, sometimes uses language in a way that some students might initially see as "unpoetic": it

140

is straightforward, simple, accessible, vivid but not ornate, compact but not dense. This poem has the quality of a speech in its repetition of points, like the problem of feeding children and like wanting men to take women seriously. Griffin also uses syntactical repetition: "who. . ."; "not . . ."; and "I like to think. . ." The poem gives us a portrait of Harriet Tubman in stanza one and the first half of stanza four and a portrait of the men "in paneled offices" in stanzas two and three; Griffin lets her argument emerge from the contrast and from the application to her own concerns — feeding children and being taken seriously. Griffin says Harriet Tubman "had no use for the law/when the law was wrong"; that is usually a good place to start class discussion.

Adrienne Rich, "The Trees"

You can discuss "The Trees" and Zoline's "The Heat Death of the Universe" as well as Piercy's "What's that smell in the kitchen?" and Carson's "I Cannot Remember All the Times..." as protests from the most recent wave of feminism. Rich's poems are more indirect than either Piercy's or Carson's, in part because they were written earlier. Rich, of course, later wrote much more direct poems on this subject. The sense of entrapment and anger breaks out in indirect forms in Rich's poems and in Zoline's story, displaced onto trees and other vegetation which each of the poem's speakers seems to identify with — or at least to feel some intense concern about. Here, stanzas 1, 2, and 4 chronicle the trees' self directed uprooting as they break out of their "tamed" state and return to the wild. The third stanza brings in the curiously detached "I" of the poem, "writing long letters/in which I scarcely mention the departure/of the forest from the house." Rich says (see quote at beginning of "How Poetry Works") that poems are like dreams; in them we put what we don't know we know. How might that statement be applied to this poem?

Raymond R. Patterson, "At That Moment"

The Autobiography of Malcolm X and Spike Lee's recent film biography are obvious choices to pair with this poem if you are doing a unit on a specific political figure. Another possibility is to look at a cross-section of poems in Varieties of Protest focusing on individual people, either historical figures or not: poems by Susan Griffin (Harriet Tubman), e.e. cummings (Olaf), Pablo Neruda (Federico García Lorca), W. H.

141

Auden (unknown citizen), Robert Hayden (Frederick Douglas). What do we learn about heroism from reading these poems? What do these poems, including Patterson's, do to make the person who is the subject of the poem become a metaphor, sometimes a symbol? Here Patterson gives Malcolm's shed blood his revolutionary power, concocting a fantasy of the blood taking over the electric, gas, water systems of the city. The last line of the poem operates on two levels — both the death of Malcolm X and the revolution he might have inspired have "already happened." Why do people write poems (or prose) about people who have died (eulogies)? What are the personal and communal functions of such writings?

Marge Piercy, "What's that smell in the kitchen?"

Piercy offers a feminist reinterpretation of a common phenomenon; women students who are or have been married (or living with a man) should have a lot to say about this poem. You might focus discussion for a while on that "supposed to" in line 7 — what are some of the sources of the pressure to bring dinner "with calico/smile on platters glittering like wax"? Are students surprised when, in lines 20 and 21, Piercy defines the woman's complaint so narrowly?

Allen Ginsberg, "America"

How does the poet's position as someone outside the mainstream of American society (as a poet, as a gay man, as a leftist) shape the way he sees America and his relation to it? You could compare the speaker's view of America with Smith's view of England in "The Loneliness of the Long-distance Runner." You could also consider this poem along with protest poems by lesbian poets Pat Parker and Judy Grahn in this section. Bob Dylan's song "With God on Our Side" (in "Peace and War") presents a view of Americans' relation with their country that might work well with Ginsberg's poem. In the middle of the poem Ginsberg writes, "It occurs to me that I am America," and he then addresses the next stanza to himself. Aside from the humor, what effect does this have? Toward the end of the poem, right after "America, it's them bad Russians," Ginsberg drops into a few deliberately illiterate lines. What is his purpose here and what is the effect? You could discuss what the speaker of the poem concludes his job is that he'd "better get right down to."

John Greenleaf Whittier, "For Righteousness' Sake"

Whittier was a Quaker and an abolitionist agitator. Being religious for him meant battling injustice, not paying "tithes for soul-insurance." Students might be asked how accurately the first stanza describes our own times and also whether there is any contradiction between the sentiments expressed in the first stanza and the last. This poem might be read with Robert Lowell's "For the Union Dead" and, for an interesting contrast, with Bob Dylan's song "With God on Our Side" in the "Peace and War" section.

Ralph Chaplin, song: "Solidarity Forever"

Students familiar only with today's labor unions may need to be told about a more militant and optimistic era in union history, an era when talk of bringing "to birth the new world from the ashes of the old" was truly compelling. (Ralph Chaplin edited the IWW paper Solidarity.) The question — "Who built the seven gates of Thebes?" — asked in Brecht's poem "A Worker Reads History" in the "Money and Work" section is answered quite decisively in this song.

William Butler Yeats, "Easter 1916"

The speaker's attitude towards the revolutionaries (who after all act on his belief as well as theirs in the cause of Irish independence) remains rather detached. But it does change over the course of the poem, and students might be asked to trace its evolution — as well as to explore all the implications of that "stone." Students might also want to talk about how they feel towards people who actively protest, take risks — undoubtedly less dramatic than those in the poem — on behalf of causes that they (the students) also believe in, but do not act on.

143

Claude McKay, "If We Must Die"

Roughly a hundred black people a year were lynched in the United States in the decades around the turn of the century — not to mention uncounted lesser acts of violence, and the continuous physical and psychological violence of poverty and racism. Knowing this, students (especially white students) might be more likely to understand McKay's passion, his talk of killing and dying. What's the effect of so bold a statement in sonnet form? Why does the speaker wish that the "monsters" be "constrained to honor us"? Why wish to be honored by monsters?

e.e. cummings, "i sing of Olaf glad and big"

One of the most striking things about this poem about individual protest by a conscientious objector is the contrast between the lighthearted rhythms and cummings's characteristic plays with language on the one hand and the brutal torturing of Olaf that the poem depicts on the other. Ask students to discuss the last line; why does cummings say Olaf was "more brave than me: more blond than you"? How far would most people go, how much would most people take, to express their convictions?

Pablo Neruda, "Ode to Federico García Lorca"

Perhaps the greatest poet writing in Spanish in the twentieth century, Neruda received the Nobel Prize for literature in 1971. He was at different times in his life both a diplomat for Chile and an exile from Chile. His poetry is infused with his radical politics; he writes in his Memoirs that he sees himself as the poet of his people. His Memoirs, by the way, are wonderful both in themselves and as a supplement to his poetry, which is available in English in Selected Poems of Pablo Neruda and Residence on Earth.

Some discussion and study questions: 1) This poem is divided into three major parts. Try to identify where each begins and ends and what each is doing. 2) Neruda's ode is a poem of tribute from one poet to another. What do we learn from Neruda about Lorca's poetry, about what kind of poetry it is and how it affects Neruda? 3) What is the tone of this poem? Does it consist of a mixture of emotions? Suggestion: you might analyze the four-line opening stanza. 4) What does Neruda suggest is the function of poetry —"what are verses for. . ."? In this context, you might look at the quote from Neruda at the beginning of "How Poetry Works."

Possible writing exercises: 1) Neruda's images here are more associative and dream-like than they are "realistic." Choose two or three images in the poem and explore the associations and emotions they evoke in you. 2) Lorca was a poet writing against fascism during the Spanish Civil War. He was executed a year after this poem was written. Does knowing this affect your reading of the poem? Comment on any tragic ironies in the poem highlighted by this fact. 3) Read Lorca's "Ballad of the Spanish Civil Guard" (in "Peace and War") and comment on the connections between the two poems in language, imagery, emotion.

W.H. Auden, "The Unknown Citizen"

This heavily ironic poem protests a soulless, bureaucratic, mechanical, conformist, manipulated society by depicting a character, an ideal citizen, who never protested. Students should easily be able to see how rhyme, rhythm, and tone serve Auden's purposes. "Was he free? Was he happy?" These questions are worth pursuing. Students might also discuss what today's version of the unknown citizen would be like — certainly more of a consumer than in this 1940 poem.

Robert Hayden, "Frederick Douglass"

The long, periodic first sentence of this poem —its main verb is withheld until line 11 — builds majestically, suggesting the power and sweep of Douglass's vision of freedom. Of course, along with his "visioning" went a life of protest — his escape from slavery, his activities as an abolitionist writer and speaker, his work organizing black Union regiments during the Civil War.

Langston Hughes, "Harlem"

There is a fairly extensive discussion of the sound and imagery of "Harlem" in "How Poetry Works." "Harlem" is one of the most famous poems in Hughes's 1951 book-length sequence, <u>Montage of a Dream Deferred</u>. Lorraine Hansberry borrowed the phrase "raisin in the sun" for the title of her play. There are a couple of excellent tapes of Langston Hughes reading his poems, including "Harlem," and discussing his poetics.

Wole Soyinka, "Telephone Conversation"

The situation in the poem — looking for an apartment and trying to convince a prospective landlady that you'd be a desirable tenant — ought to be familiar and easy to identify with for many students. How does Soyinka characterize the prospective landlady? How about the prospective tenant? What is the effect of our hearing only one side of the conversation, as he repeats her words and responds to them? How does this help Soyinka achieve the good-natured and humorous tone of the poem? How does it help us both identify with the speaker and see how ridiculous racism is?

Sylvia Plath, "Daddy"

One of Plath's most famous and angriest poems, "Daddy" frequently evokes stunned silence in students hearing the poem for the first time. There is a tape of Plath reading this poem along with "Lady Lazarus" and "Fever 103" on a series of tapes of British poets, edited by Peter Orr, <u>The Poet Speaks</u>. The poem is a kind of exorcism of the various avatars of Daddy —the black shoe, the ghastly statue, the panzer-man or Nazi, the teacher (an actual image of her professor father), the devil, the husband (the man in black with a meinkampf look), and finally the vampire who is both husband and father. The villagers help her kill the vampire, a communal action unusual in Plath's poems. The rhythm of the poem is incantational, powerful and pounding in its childlike rhythms and rhymes, its repetitive sound of you, do, two, Jew, true, shoe, screw, glue, I'm through. Pairs well with Joy Harjo's "I Give You Back," which is also incantational in form and intent but has a different tone.

Ray Durem, "To the pale poets"

Durem brings up the question of how one writes poetry about the brutality of violent death or about tedious backbreaking jobs like domestic labor. Students might discuss what their expectations about poetry are: do they expect, as Durem suggests, that poetry will be obscure, filled with fine and subtle feelings, with melody and pretty images? You might ask students to pick an "unpoetic" subject and write a few lines of poetry about it.

Peggy Seeger, song: "I'm Gonna Be an Engineer"

The lyrics of Seeger's song fit with themes raised in both the "Money and Work" and the "Women and Men" sections. Try to get a recording of the song, which shows the different intonations she uses in different parts of the song, for example, in the three parts of stanza one. What the speaker of the poem has to contend are with all the voices — her mother, her teachers, her husband, her boss — that consistently oppose her ambition and try to wear her down. A more pervasive voice, of the culture as a whole, comes in the capitalized sections ("DAINTY AS A DRESDEN STATUE. . .). As an example of how women are socialized, this could be compared to Jamaica Kincaid's "Girl" and the excerpt from Morrison's The Bluest Eye in "Growing Up and Growing Older."

Judy Grahn, "A Woman Is Talking To Death"

Originally published separately as a long poem, "A Woman Is Talking to Death" is included in Grahn's collection of her first five books, The Work of a Common Woman. A lesbian feminist poet from a working class background, Grahn has been an important force, from the late 60s on, in developing a feminist small press movement. See comments about this poem in the preface to this section. Why is the woman talking to eath; what does Death represent; what are its characteristics in this poem?

Section One: the accident on the bridge; the police and their intimidation of the Black man; the question of witnessing. See lines 141-144. Also go back to the opening three lines and discuss why Grahn begins with the juxtaposition of "testimony in trials that never got heard" and the wonderful two line image of her lover's teeth, her lover's muscles that is repeated throughout the poem. See line 135 ("and no child in them"); this image recurs also.

Section Two: Who is death? This section also picks up the theme in lines 141-144 of the previous section.

Section Three: three incidents — being a nurse's aide, being kicked out of the military for being a lesbian, the story about the soldiers who blindly follow their orders and drown in defective amphibian tanks. How do these three fit together?

Section Four: Who is interrogating the speaker? How does she subvert the questions, so that they make a statement of commitment and involvement with people that becomes a philosophy to set against death. The story of Josie.

Section Five: How women are constrained and hemmed in because they are seen as prey. How are lines 357-365 an answer? And what good does living "safely" do? — "death breaks in the window." The story about the adulterous woman and the mouse.

Section Six: How oppressed groups oppress each other. The Spanish man who calls her queer and beats her up; the police who laugh. Josie reappears.

Section Seven: The story of the woman who had been raped and beaten. They comfort her but leave her to the police with no child in them. The judgment about how we abandon people "much too soon to get the real loving done."

Section Eight: Another mock interrogation, this time of the woman abused in section seven.

Section Nine: The concluding section — what is the best way to fight against Death? Has the meaning of Death been enlarged in this poem?

Pat Parker, "Where Will You Be?"

"Where Will You Be?" is in particular about the oppression of homosexuals, but the speaker's rhetorical question — "where will you be when they come?" — could be asked of members of most oppressed groups. Specifically, Parker directs her question not at the oppressors but at those members of the oppressed group who, out of fear or self-protectiveness, don't stand up to be counted. She gives several examples and everyone can identify with one time or another when they didn't stand up for their convictions, didn't support someone who was being harassed. Parker further implies, as Grahn does in "A Woman is Talking to Death" and Susan Griffin does in "I Like to Think of Harriet Tubman," that the forms of oppression can be quite legal: "They will come/in business suits/to buy your homes/and bring bodies to/fill your jobs." As Grahn redefines heroism, love, death in "A Woman is Talking to Death," Parker redefines "perverse" in this poem.

Linda Hogan, "Black Hills Survival Gathering, 1980"

Linda Hogan, herself a Chickasaw, has written about a weeks-long protest against the continuing encroachment of military development onto traditional lands. Jarring juxtapositions of the natural and the technological ("Dry grass blows from their hair./B52's blow over their heads.") dramatize the clash between two ways of life. The middle two stanzas of the poem offer a peaceful scene of family life in the midst of threatening forces; B52's above them and bombs "buried beneath" them, the speaker and her husband lovingly care for their children, who so obviously need the kind of protection they, not military machinery, can offer. The morning with her family seems to give the speaker hope: the horse at first "looks like one burned/over Hiroshima," but then "raises her head/and surges toward the bluing sky"; the men in orange cloth who had appeared "on fire" are now "singing and drumming." It's a "Radiant morning" and the protest may very well succeed.

Joy Harjo, "The Woman Hanging From the Thirteenth Floor Window"

You might begin discussing the poem by asking students to list everything they are told or can infer about this woman. She seems not to be one of "the rich"; she has three children; she is apparently responsible for them all by herself; and so on. The next question to ask is why she's out there, hanging from the thirteenth floor window. In the last stanza we're told she's "crying for/the lost beauty of her own life." Exactly what's been lost? And how? The woman hanging seems to represent many women, at least many poor women: "She is all of the women of the apartment/building who stand watching her, watching themselves." She has been living not for herself but for others, defined by the needs of others: she's the mother of her children as well as "her mother's daughter and her father's son." Hanging from the thirteenth floor window is an act of protest, a desperate effort "to claim herself again."

Joy Harjo, "I Give You Back"

An incantation to free oneself from fear — a fear that is personally and historically based. Ask students to list what the speaker of the poem has been afraid of. How does she say she has participated in imprisoning herself in fear? What method does she use to free herself finally from fear? Students could compare this poem to Sylvia Plath's "Daddy," also an incantation to release oneself from the oppressive weight of the past. Judy Grahn's "A Woman Is Talking To Death" has a similar set of conclusions about fear as Harjo's poem. See Harjo's other poems included in this anthology: "The Woman Hanging from the Thirteenth Floor Window" in this section, "Remember" in Growing Up and Growing Older, and "Resurrection" in Peace and War. The PBS series on American poets by Bill Moyers has a 15-minute segment on Joy Harjo which includes her reading "I Give You Back."

Jo Carson, "I Cannot Remember All the Times..."

Pairs well with almost any week's newspaper stories about the latest murder of a woman by her husband or boyfriend. Beatings of women are so common these days they're not even reported. Any latest statistics you can find on domestic violence of women by men will help in teaching this poem, which may arouse strong denial among many male and some female students who won't want to believe how often the situation in this poem happens. The protest in this poem is, really, to finally break silence about the abuse and to advise other women (what, specifically, is her advice?) to do the same and, having broken silence, to leave before it happens again — because "he loves you hurt/and he will hit you again." You might ask students to trace the progression of violence in this relationship. Sandra Cisneros's story "Woman Hollering Creek" treats the same theme of domestic violence and works well with this poem.

DRAMA

Sophocles, <u>Antigone</u>

Who is the tragic center of this play? The protagonist (Antigone) and the antagonist (Creon) are exceptionally well balanced in <u>Antigone</u>. They both possess the tragic flaw of hubris or pride; they both believe they are right. However, Antigone dies and Creon is left to suffer the loss of his son and his wife and his political support and finally to come to the realization that he was wrong. Creon does develop as a character and achieve some inner change, though it comes too late to help him. Antigone, on the other hand, is the character with whom most readers sympathize; she is traditionally heroic, idealistic, selfless, and passionate while Creon seems to be motivated solely by considerations of power, of consolidating his new regime. That may be why he reacts so strongly to Antigone's symbolic burial of her brother; with both of Antigone and Ismene's brothers dead, the sisters are all that is left of the previous royal family and are therefore a threat to Creon's power.

As we mentioned in the study questions, Antigone and Creon's conflict has four key dimensions: youth vs. age, individual vs. the state, religious vs. secular, and female vs. male. Creon assumes everyone is motivated, like he is, by power hunger and/or greed and so he cannot understand the idealism and need to adhere to religious tradition that motivates Antigone. He is also annoyed with both Antigone and Haemon for defying his parental and quasi-parental authority, for presuming to correct someone older than they and in a position of authority over them. Creon is further outraged that a woman (and when Ismene joins Antigone, two women) should presume to defy him. As do many of the pieces in this section, <u>Antigone</u> concerns as well the conflict between the individual and the state. Here the state is personified in Creon, which in some ways makes the philosophical issue less complex for modern readers, since we can see very clearly Creon's political motivations and his political incompetence in overreacting to Antigone's wish to see both brothers buried decently.

Antigone, like Olaf in e.e. cummings's poem in this section, like John Woolman and Thoreau (see nonfiction, this section), is acting as an individual and out of personal conviction. She acts out of what she believes to be right. It is a choice; she knows the consequences, but she cannot do anything but what she does. Another view of Antigone, of course, is that she is just as pig-headed stubborn as Creon, and that by knowingly committing a capital crime in Thebes, she has selfishly chosen to leave behind an unhappy a sister and a fiancé who love her. Another way to see her is as someone who is as politically aware as Creon. Indeed, had she not been a woman, she would have become ruler of Thebes. Perhaps she is indeed what Creon in part thinks — a nucleus for an anti-Creon faction in Thebes, a power base to knock him off his throne or, at the least, to make ruling Thebes more difficult. Yet another approach might see her as suicidal from the beginning and trying, consciously or not, to achieve her own death. All of these possibilities and more can come up in a discussion of <u>Antigone</u>. Also you might ask students to consider the opinions of Tiresius, of Haemon, and of the citizens of Thebes in the choral odes.

Alice Childress, "Florence"

Students reading "Florence" may not be very aware of the not so distant history of legal segregation. You might spend some time, using details in the play, piecing together (and filling out) the picture. Mama won't be permitted to go to the "diner" on the train, for example; the station waiting room itself is segregated (note "<u>women</u>" vs. "<u>ladies</u>" and "<u>men</u>" vs. "<u>gentlemen</u>" in the opening stage directions); Florence's husband Jim "got killed at voting time." The impact of white power on the lives of black people is suggested by the way things change when Mrs. Carter shows up: Mama and the Porter have been talking pleasantly, respectfully addressing each other as "Mrs. Whitney" and "Mr. Brown," when suddenly Mr. Brown, who is about fifty and has a son in college, is called "Boy" and told to fetch the bags. The often comic figure of Mrs. Carter illustrates the inadequacy (to say the least) of white liberal sympathy. She feels superior to the racist South, with its "silly laws"; she's sent $1,000 "to a Negro college for scholarships"; and she's even "eaten with Negroes." But she can only see Florence as a domestic, not as an actress. However 'well-meaning' she may or may not be (something probably worth discussing), Mrs. Carter can't help but be patronizing. White society does not only oppress black people, but insists on defining them and their experience as well. Mrs. Carter's brother Jeff, the novelist who "knows the Negro so well," can only envision his heroine Zelma as tragic or pathetic. Mama, by deciding to support Florence's aspirations to the fullest extent she can, is asserting her daughter's right to define herself. The difficulty, and the necessity, of Mama's act of protest should not be underestimated.

NONFICTION

John Woolman, from The Journal of John Woolman

The Society of Friends (Quakers) was begun in England in the mid-17th century by George Fox. It was considered a radical form of Protestantism for a number of reasons: Friends saw no need for a Church establishment and hierarchy or for ordained ministers. They believed that God existed in each person as "a light within" and, when a group of Friends was gathered in silent worship, that God was there. They saw no need for designated ministers, since anyone who felt "moved to speak" during Meeting could stand up and speak into the silence. They believed that each person interpreted the scriptures for him or herself. They believed in gender equality in religious matters. They did not believe in social hierarchy and often found themselves in trouble for refusing to follow such social forms as taking off their hats to members of the upper classes. They were pacifists and refused to serve in the military. They believed in a frugal, unostentatious, "unworldly" lifestyle. Persecuted in England, many emigrated to the U.S., where they became quite successful in business. The only literary forms unworldly enough to merit their approval in the 17th and 18th centuries were letters and journals. A number of Friends kept journals, of which John Woolman's is the best known.

Woolman's statement, "it is the duty of all to be firm in that which they certainly know is right for them," comes directly out of the Quaker belief that God is located not out there somewhere but in each person, that each person is an authoritative source of truth. In the excerpts from his Journal included here, Woolman acts out his antislavery convictions by: refusing to write wills for people who are passing on slaves as property, by refusing to accept free hospitality from those who live off slave labor, and by arguing as eloquently as he can against slaveholding whenever he gets the chance. Since even among Friends in the 18th century there were many slaveholders, Woolman often found himself having to speak up against and to people of some weight in the community and he talks about how hard that was.

Henry David Thoreau, "Civil Disobedience"

See the brief discussion of "Civil Disobedience" in "How Nonfiction Works." Compare Thoreau's remark that "the only obligation which I have a right to assume is to do at any time what I think right" with John Woolman's "it is the duty of all to be firm in that which they certainly know is right for them" and ask students to discuss this concept of individual conscience. What will probably emerge in the discussion is a fear that this philosophy leads to a general lawlessness, and examples of criminal and other antisocial behavior will be brought up. What do both Woolman and Thoreau assume about the individual that allows each of them to make such a statement?

Something with which Woolman is not concerned in the excerpt from his Journal and Thoreau definitely is in his essay is systems of power such as government. After discussing what Thoreau thinks is wrong with government, you could go on to envision what Thoreau's ideal form of governing would be and what would be necessary in order for that to work. See his concluding paragraph. If one's conscience will not support some action of one's government, then Thoreau tells us we should not support it in practice, by for example not paying that portion of our taxes which would pay for that action. Or by withdrawing in other practical ways from a social contract which we find unjust or oppressive. Consider Susan Griffin's remark in "I Like to Think of Harriet Tubman" that Harriet Tubman "had no use for the law/when the law was wrong."

Thoreau's essay is in part concerned with the consequences of such action. Since the state can harass the objecting individual, it is better, Thoreau says, not to accumulate property. "You must live within yourself, and depend upon yourself, always tucked up and ready for a start, and not have many affairs." Another cost is being thrown in jail, and the nutmeat of this essay is Thoreau's account of his night in jail. Thoreau's night in prison seems relatively benign: does that undercut his argument at all? He implies it's not his concern if someone else pays his tax. Do students agree? Thoreau writes: "Under a government which imprisons any unjustly, the true place for a just man is also a prison." Thoreau speaks of judging from a lower, a higher, and a highest perspective (with which Woolman would probably agree). He follows this with a remark about freedom which students might want to debate: "If a man is thought-free, fancy-free, imagination-free. . . unwise rulers or reformers cannot fatally interrupt him."

Harriet Jacobs, from <u>Incidents in the Life of a Slave Girl</u>

This excerpt is from one of the hundreds of slave narratives that were published, usually in an effort to advance the abolitionist cause. Jacobs tells her own individual story, but her aim is to awaken readers to the evils of the institution of slavery. Her writing represents, as she says in the preface to the book, an "effort in behalf of my persecuted people." We don't witness the full range of horrors of slavery, as Jacobs herself points out; we don't see the backbreaking <u>labor</u> which was of course the whole reason for slavery; and the fragments here don't have the cumulative effect the whole book has. But we do get a sense, for example, of family life under slavery — of the intensity of the emotional bonds between family members, as in Jacobs's longing for her children and in her relationship with her grandmother, and also of the cruel way in which families are broken up, as when Fanny and her children are sold to different masters. In addition, we get a strong sense of the sexual exploitation and abuse women slaves were subjected to. Jacobs's language in describing her treatment at the hands of Dr. Flint is at once intense and veiled, an indication of her great need to say what usually was left unsaid. The most significant form of protest for slaves was flight, a difficult and risky undertaking; seven years of hiding in an attic was a price worth paying for a chance at freedom. You might ask students what they would have done in a similar situation.

Thomas S. Whitecloud, "Blue Winds Dancing"

Some students may really take to Whitecloud's critique of "civilization" — the rat race, the irrelevance of college, the alienation and materialism — and may find his vision of a community of serene and simple people, in tune with nature and with each other, very appealing. Encourage them to articulate their feelings and to try to explain, for example, what Whitecloud means when he says "civilized white men" (women are nearly invisible in this essay) are "always dissatisfied," or when he speaks of "a city sucking life from all the country around." But don't let escape unnoticed the hints of his ambivalence and discomfort, the way, for example, his "throat tightens" as he watches his sister "save carefully bits of red string from the packages." Life is difficult on Indian reservations; the history of genocidal policy toward Native Americans did not end happily for the survivors. "Funny that my people should be ever falling farther behind," Whitecloud writes. "The more they try to imitate whites the more tragic the result. . . About all we imitate well are their vices." The switch here from "they" to "we" suggests the difficulty Whitecloud has fully identifying with his people. His essay seems to move from his aloneness at school, on to some small companionship with the "bums," and finally to joyous integration with his community as he joins the dance at the end — but Whitecloud remains, inevitably, significantly more troubled than his very neat last sentence suggests.

Martin Luther King, Jr., "I Have a Dream"

Most students will probably have seen film clips of King delivering this speech; if not, you might want at least to let them hear his voice. But even on paper, the speech works. King's metaphors are clear and powerful (and they offer a good occasion to discuss or review the way metaphors work). The many rich metaphors help ground what, at least in its first half, is really a very abstract speech. The often cited metaphor of the promissory note and "bad check" highlights the economic aspects of racism and also seems to turn on its head racist stereotypes about financial irresponsibility. Since it is a speech, "I Have a Dream" uses parallelism and repetition frequently. The repetition, for example, of "now is the time" early on not only structures a long sentence for easier aural comprehension, but also hammers home "the urgency of the moment." And of course there is the repetition of "I have a dream." Mindful, perhaps, of his wider audience, King speaks patriotically — he echoes Lincoln ("Fivescore years"), he quotes at length from a patriotic song, and at the end he catalogues the nation's natural beauties. He also manages to remind listeners that violence threatens while at the same time advising against it. You might ask students what would need to be different if such a speech were to be delivered today.